Nationalism and Ethnic Conflict

Nationalism and Ethnic Conflict

Class, State, and Nation in the Age of Globalization

Berch Berberoglu

ROWMAN & LITTLEFIELD PUBLISHERS, INC.
Lanham • Boulder • New York • Toronto • Oxford

ROWMAN & LITTLEFIELD PUBLISHERS, INC.

Published in the United States of America
by Rowman & Littlefield Publishers, Inc.
A wholly owned subsidiary of The Rowman & Littlefield Publishing Group, Inc.
4501 Forbes Boulevard, Suite 200, Lanham, Maryland 20706
www.rowmanlittlefield.com

PO Box 317
Oxford, OX2 9RU, UK

British Library Cataloguing in Publication Information Available

Library of Congress Cataloging-in-Publication Data

Berberoglu, Berch.
  Nationalism and ethnic conflict : class, state, and nation in the
age of globalization / Berch Berberoglu.
    p. cm.
  Includes bibliographical references and index.
  ISBN 0-7425-3543-6 (hardcover : alk. paper)
  1. Nationalism. 2. Ethnic conflict. 3. Globalization. I. Title.
  JC311.B43 2004
  320.54—dc22

                                            2004003412

Printed in the United States of America

⊗™ The paper used in this publication meets the minimum requirements of American National Standard for Information Sciences—Permanence of Paper for Printed Library Materials, ANSI/NISO Z39.48-1992.

Contents

Preface

As the twentieth century came to a close with the monumental changes that we witnessed during the decade of the 1990s, the world community saw a remarkable rise and spread of nationalism and ethnic conflict, which have come to pose a new challenge to interstate relations in the age of globalization. The relationship between class, state, and nation has become a major factor across a spectrum of global political–economic events at the end of the twentieth and beginning of the twenty-first century. Nationalism has been at the core of this relationship since the formation of nation-states in the late eighteenth century and has come to pose a renewed challenge to society in the epoch of global capitalism.

My interest in nationalism and ethnonational conflict goes back nearly a quarter of a century when in the mid-1970s I set out to study the origins and development of nationalism in Turkey as part of my doctoral dissertation project, which later resulted in the publication of my first book, *Turkey in Crisis: From State Capitalism to Neo-Colonialism* (London: Zed Press, 1982). This was complemented by a series of graduate seminars on imperialism and national liberation, as well as the political economy of class, state, and revolution, conducted by Albert J. Szymanski in the sociology department at the University of Oregon between 1974 and 1977.

In the mid-1980s, I published a collection of historical writings on nationalism and the struggle against British imperialism in India titled *India: National Liberation and Class Struggle* (Meerut, India: Sarup and Sons Publishers, 1985), focusing on the history of anti-imperialist national struggles in an important region of the Third World. While issues surrounding nationalism, the national question, and ethnonational conflict have been prominent in much of my writings over the past twenty-five years, the publication of my book *The*

National Question: Nationalism, Ethnic Conflict, and Self-Determination in the Twentieth Century (Philadelphia: Temple University Press, 1995) and my more recent work culminating in this present book, *Nationalism and Ethnic Conflict: Class, State, and Nation in the Age of Globalization*, have come to highlight what is now clearly a major worldwide phenomenon.

Today, nationalism is more widespread and more pervasive than any other social force intent on transforming society. And today, nationalism has become the battle cry of progressive and reactionary forces alike—in the first world as well as in the Third World, and in the former socialist states of Eastern Europe and the former Soviet Union.

Why? Why has this seemingly dormant or declining phenomenon in recent times gained another lease on life in the age of globalization and transnationalization of the world political economy, culture, and society? Why the renewed revival for national identity, nationalist ideology, and ethnonational conflict, war, and bloodshed that we see all around us? What is the nature of these movements, who (which class or classes) are behind their activities and providing them support, and which social forces (including the media, religious groups, and, above all, the state) are at work fostering national divisions, national antagonisms, and ethnonational conflicts to protect and advance established class interests or support newly rising class forces that would benefit in the quest for further global class domination? Finally, how do class, state, and nation interact and articulate to affect and shape the nature and dynamics of nationalism and ethnic conflict that have brought this problem to the forefront of social scientific inquiry?

It is to provide some answers to these and related questions, and thus to contribute to our understanding of nationalism and ethnic conflict, that this book was conceived and written. This volume, which brings to fruition two decades of analysis and reflection on the question of nationalism and ethnonational conflict, serves as a much needed corrective to dominant, conventional approaches to this important problem that is at once political, economic, cultural, and, above all, social. A class-based perspective on nationalism, as I provide here, thus makes a major contribution to the discussion and debate on the nature, dynamics, and contradictions of this all-pervasive phenomenon.

Acknowledgments

No piece of intellectual work that covers such a vast topic and area of study as nationalism and ethnic conflict can emerge through the knowledge and efforts of a single individual alone. This book is, therefore, a product of a collective effort that incorporates the works of many others, and thus has been influenced by the thinking of many individuals, some like minded and others not.

I would like to thank, first and foremost, my mentor Al Szymanski, who, more than anyone else, taught me in the clearest terms the class nature of nationalism, racism, patriarchy, and other forms of oppression, which to many still seem to be a mystery and a puzzle. Al's teachings and ideas have contributed to the intellectual development of a whole generation of critical intellectuals who, despite the adversities that shadow intellectual life in academia today, continue to uphold these ideas and principles in an uncompromising way.

Others, including Larry Reynolds, James Petras, and Blain Stevenson, have also been an inspiration in my intellectual work. From early on, they have helped me understand and expose the hidden dimensions of social life that often go unnoticed. I thank them for providing me a solid base for further scholarly work.

In exploring the vast literature and spectrum of ideas on nationalism, national movements, and ethnonational conflict over a number of years, a view and an understanding of the topic has emerged that informs the present study. In this context, I would like to thank James Petras, Alan Spector, Gianfranco Pala, Carla Filosa, Marty Orr, Harutyun Marutyan, Johnson Makoba, Viktoria Hertling, and David Lott for their contribution to discussions on some very important issues surrounding the phenomenon of nationalism.

This book has benefited from two graduate seminars that I conducted on nationalism and the state as visiting professor of political economy at the Institute of Political Economy, Carleton University, Ottawa, Canada, during the summers of 1997 and 1998, as well as three advanced undergraduate courses that I taught on Third World development and political sociology as visiting professor of sociology at the University of Victoria, British Columbia, Canada, during the summers of 1999 and 2000. I would like to thank Michael Dolan, former director of the Institute of Political Economy at Carleton, for inviting me to conduct one of these seminars, and Wally Clement, the subsequent director of the institute, for inviting me back the following year to conduct another seminar there. My thanks also go to Rennie Warburton, then chair of the sociology department at the University of Victoria, for inviting me to teach three other courses at UVIC during the following two summers. Most importantly, I would like to thank my students in these seminars and courses, as well as several others that I normally teach at my own university, the University of Nevada, Reno, who have actively participated in these seminars and courses and have thus made a significant contribution to the shaping of this project, which is reflected in the various pages of this book.

Several trips to Eastern Europe, the Balkans, the former Soviet republics, China, the Middle East (including the West Bank, Israel, Egypt, Cyprus, and Lebanon), North Africa, and Central and South America between 1995 and 2003 conferring with colleagues on issues related to nationalism and ethnic conflict further contributed to my understanding of nationalism and national movements around the world.

This book emerged as part of my University of Nevada, Reno, Foundation Professorship research project in the late 1990s, which has generated two books, several articles, and a number of presentations at national and international conferences around the world, and was completed during my sabbatical leave in 2003. I would like to thank the University of Nevada, Reno, Foundation and the Professional Development Leave Committee for providing me the opportunity to carry out and complete this project. My thanks go to Ann Ronald, former dean of the college of Arts and Science at the University of Nevada, Reno, for nominating me to receive this prestigious award as Foundation Professor, and to Bob Mead, subsequent dean of the college, for his encouragement and support of my efforts in pursuing my scholarship during my tenure as department chair for nearly a decade throughout the 1990s until 2001, when my fourth term as chair ended.

Finally, I would like to thank my wife, Suzan, and my sons, Stephen and Michael, for their continued support and understanding in helping me accomplish my intellectual work.

Needless to say, the ideas expressed and the analyses provided in this book are mine alone, and thus I alone bear responsibility for their accuracy and interpretation.

Introduction

During the final decade of the twentieth century, the global community witnessed the remarkable growth and spread of nationalism and ethnic conflict. In the first, inaugural issue of *Nations and Nationalism*, the journal of the Association for the Study of Ethnicity and Nationalism, published in 1995, the editors, Anthony Smith et al. wrote:

> The last few years have witnessed a widespread resurgence of nationalism and proliferation of ethnic conflicts. The reemergence of ethnic nationalisms across the globe has taken many people by surprise and forced them to reassess prevailing assumptions and beliefs about the direction of historical development and the motive forces of social change. In longer historical perspective, the latest resurgence of nationalism is one of many since the French Revolution which have propelled the nation into the forefront of world politics. Given the unsatisfied aspirations of ethnic communities in many parts of the world, it is unlikely that the present wave of nationalisms will be the final one.[1]

Today, as we leave the twentieth century behind us, movements for national liberation and autonomy have become a worldwide phenomenon, spreading to distant corners of the world—from the Middle East to southern Africa, to Eastern and Western Europe, to North America, and to the former Soviet Union.[2] The recent transformations in Eastern Europe and the former Soviet Union, especially the Balkans and the Transcaucasian region, have fueled the upsurge in national rivalries and led to ethnic conflict and civil war that now stretches across the globe.[3]

This book examines the origins and development of nationalism and national movements in the twentieth century and provides an analysis of the nature and dynamics of nationalism and ethnic conflict in a variety of national settings. Examining the intricate relationship between class, state, and nation, this book attempts to develop a critical approach to the study of nationalism and national movements within the broader context of class relations and class struggles in the age of globalization.[4]

Originating in Europe in a period when the rising European bourgeoisie in the eighteenth century found it necessary to establish nation-states to protect their economic interests and thus consolidate their class rule, the phenomenon of nation (and nationalism) became the political expression of rival capitalist powers engaged in a life-and-death struggle for world domination throughout the eighteenth and nineteenth centuries.[5]

In the twentieth century, nationalism and national movements emerged across much of the world as rallying points in the context of the struggle against European colonialism and imperialism.[6] National struggles against foreign domination in Asia, Africa, and the Middle East, for example, have taken the form of anticolonial or anti-imperialist liberation struggles—as in India and China in the 1940s, in Algeria and Cuba in the 1950s, and in much of sub-Saharan Africa in the 1960s and 1970s.[7] In these and other countries and regions of the Third World subjected to external domination, the yearning for national independence and self-determination has taken the form of political struggles to establish sovereign national states with jurisdiction over a national territory based on self-rule.

During the past century, we have seen nationalist movements develop in a variety of settings—in the Third World, in the advanced capitalist countries, and under socialism—varying in accordance with different geographic, historical, and cultural settings.[8] "Taking the century as a whole," write Geoff Eley and Ronald Grigor Suny, "nationalism has come in waves, crashing across the ruins of empires."[9]

> When the great multinational states of the nineteenth century fell apart, transforming the landscapes of eastern Europe, central Asia, and the Near East after 1917, not only were new nation-states formed in their debris, but nationalism itself became an object of academic study in the interwar years, conducted under the sign of a new validating norm, the self-determination of peoples. But this generally positive valence of nationalism in the first postwar decade dissipated rapidly before the rise of fascism, with its expansionist drives and attendant excess, its chauvinism and privileging of race. Something resembling the euphoria of national self-determination in 1917–18 then accompanied the end of the Second World War, as the European peoples cast off the Nazi occupation, while another wave of interest in nationalism and nation-forming rose from the slow collapse of the great European overseas empires in the decades after 1945.[10]

In the postwar period, Third World national liberation movements appeared in several forms: secular political struggles for a homeland (as in

Palestine); struggles for regional and cultural autonomy and self-rule across several states (as in Kurdistan); struggles to end racism and national oppression (as in apartheid South Africa); and ethnoreligious conflict in a multinational setting (as in India).[11] A multitude of national, political, cultural, and religious conflicts in the context of larger regional military confrontations have surfaced even in generally tolerant secular states, such as Lebanon, where the resurgence of national, ethnic, and fundamentalist religious movements have led to social strife and civil war.[i]

In the advanced capitalist countries, movements of previously colonized peoples and territories (such as Puerto Rico) and of oppressed groups and nationalities (as in Northern Ireland, the Basque Country, and Quebec) have emerged and developed during this century, especially during the past several decades. In this setting, the struggles of minority ethnic groups have tended to focus on limited autonomy and self-rule that recognizes ethnic, cultural, linguistic, and historic rights and freedoms within the context of a federated state with minimal political control over the affairs of the minority ethnic population by dominant groups in society.[12]

In the socialist countries, especially in the former Soviet Union, nationalist movements have sprung up in the Baltic, Transcaucasian, and Central Asian republics, as they have in Eastern Europe, particularly in the former Yugoslavia, where a civil war between the Serbs, the Croats, and the Bosnians has torn apart that country.[13] Here, the newly emergent nationalist forces have challenged communist rule and installed in its place a series of market-oriented bourgeois states tied to global capitalism.[14]

This book consists of three parts made up of seven chapters. In part I, chapters 1 and 2, I examine mainstream and Marxist theories of nationalism and ethnic conflict. I show that while conventional social theorists have focused on subjective factors, such as culture, ideology, religion, and other superstructural phenomena in examining the origins and development of nations and nationalism, Marxist theorists have adopted a materialist conception of history based on an analysis of the class nature of the state, nation, and nationalism in explaining the nature and transformation of superstructural phenomena that are socially defined. In contrast to mainstream, bourgeois-idealist formulations of nation and nationalism, which are viewed by conventional social theorists as an expression of free will defined in accordance with bourgeois subjectivist notions of social behavior, I show that Marxist theory, grounded in the materialist dialectic that is historically situated and guided by the logic of social relations formed by underlying class relations and class struggles, is better able to explain the structure and dynamics of society and social change, including such phenomena as nation and nationalism, and their relationship to class and state. Thus, providing a critical approach to the study of nationalism and ethnic conflict, I draw the reader's attention to the analysis provided by Marxist theory as a viable alternative to conventional modes of theorizing on class, state, nation, and nationalism.

In part II, chapters 3, 4, and 5, I examine the political context of nationalism and national movements in various national settings. Chapter 3 provides a comparative analysis of nationalism and ethnic conflict on a world scale, focusing on a variety of national movements engaged in struggles for national self-determination throughout the world. Chapter 4 examines the resurgence of nationalism in the Third World, focusing on the Palestinian and Kurdish national movements as case studies of nationalism and ethnic conflict within the context of the recent rise of Islamic fundamentalism in the Middle East. Chapter 5 looks at the rise of right-wing ultranationalist movements in the advanced capitalist countries at century's end—a development that occurred in reaction to growing racial and ethnic tensions that are a consequence of economic decline and decay resulting from the globalization of capital. Here I address the apparent paradox of the resurgence of nationalism and ethnonational conflict in the age of globalization—a process that is a direct outcome of globalization itself.

In part III, chapters 6 and 7, I address the crucial relationship between class, state, and nation—the pillars of nationalism and ethnic conflict—and provide an analysis of the social forces that serve as agents of nationalism and class struggle. In this section of the book I argue that nationalism and national movements cannot be fully understood unless the *class basis* of politics and the *class forces* behind political ideologies and mass movements are clearly revealed. In this context, I show that the state comes to play a central role in confronting various class forces and facilitates the class project of one or another of the contending classes vying for power to advance their particular class interests. A reactionary hold on power or a revolutionary transformation of existing social, economic, and political conditions thus becomes the motive force of sociopolitical relations as manifested through varied forms of class struggle that ultimately resolves the question of state power. This triangular relationship between class, state, and nation, which is organically linked to the forces of nationalism, ethnic conflict, and class struggle, explains well the dynamics of power wielded to shape and reshape society and its course of development.

The book concludes by drawing upon the theoretical and political implications of social relations that are often in conflict with various dimensions of social life. This book makes a strong case in favor of an analysis that brings into focus the dynamics of class, state, and nation to explain the class nature of nationalism and ethnic conflict in the age of globalization.

NOTES

1. Anthony Smith, Obi Igwara, Athena Leoussi, and Terry Mulhall, eds., "Editorial," *Nations and Nationalism* 1, no. 1 (1995): p. 1.

2. Berch Berberoglu, ed., *The National Question: Nationalism, Ethnic Conflict, and Self-Determination in the Twentieth Century* (Philadelphia: Temple University Press, 1995).

3. Thanasis D. Sfikas and Christopher Williams, eds., *Ethnicity and Nationalism in East Central Europe and the Balkans* (Sudbury, Mass.: Dartmouth, 1999); Misha Glenny, *The Balkans: Nationalism, War and the Great Powers 1809–1999* (New York: Penguin, 2001); Cathie Carmichael, *Ethnic Cleansing in the Balkans: Nationalism and the Destruction of Tradition* (New York: Routledge, 2002).

4. See Albert J. Szymanski, *The Capitalist State and the Politics of Class* (Cambridge, Mass.: Winthrop Publishers, 1978) and Albert J. Szymanski, *Class Structure: A Critical Perspective* (Westport, Conn.: Praeger, 1983); Berch Berberoglu, *Class Structure and Social Transformation* (Westport, Conn.: Praeger, 1994) and Berch Berberoglu, *Political Sociology: A Comparative/Historical Approach*, 2nd ed. (New York: General Hall, 2001). See also Umut Özkirimli, *Theories of Nationalism: A Critical Introduction* (New York: St. Martin's, 2000).

5. See Eric Hobsbawm, *The Age of Revolution: 1789–1848* (New York: World, 1962), chap. 7 and Eric Hobsbawm, *The Age of Capital: 1848–1875* (New York: Scribner's, 1975), chap. 5. See also Louk Hagendoorn, György Csepeli, Henk Dekker, and Russell Farnen, eds., *European Nations and Nationalism: Theoretical and Historical Perspectives* (Burlington, Vt.: Ashgate, 2000) and Anthony W. Marx, *Faith in Nation: Exclusionary Origins of Nationalism* (Oxford, U.K.: Oxford University Press, 2003).

6. For a discussion on nationalism and various nationalist movements, see James M. Blaut, *The National Question: Decolonizing the Theory of Nationalism* (London: Zed Books, 1987). See also Geoff Eley and Ronald Grigor Suny, eds., *Becoming National* (New York: Oxford University Press, 1996).

7. See Norman Miller and Roderick Aya, eds., *National Liberation: Revolution in the Third World* (New York: Free Press, 1971); Donald C. Hodges and Robert Elias Abu Shanab, eds., *NLF: National Liberation Fronts, 1960/1970* (New York: Morrow, 1972).

8. For an extended analysis of the political history of various national movements throughout the world, see Berberoglu, *The National Question*.

9. Geoff Eley and Ronald Grigor Suny, "Introduction: From the Moment of Social History to the Work of Cultural Representation," in Eley and Suny, *Becoming National*, p. 3.

10. Eley and Suny, "Introduction," p. 3.

11. Berberoglu, *The National Question*.

12. Dilip Hiro, *Lebanon: Fire and Embers; a History of the Lebanese Civil War* (New York: St. Martin's, 1993).

13. This is especially the case in Quebec, but also in Puerto Rico and the Basque Country and elsewhere in the advanced capitalist countries, as well as in parts of the

Third World, such as Kurdistan. See Michael Keating, *Nations against the State: The New Politics of Nationalism in Quebec, Catalonia, and Scotland* (London: Macmillan, 2002); William A. Douglass, Carmelo Urza, Linda White, and Joseba Zulaika, eds., *Basque Politics and Nationalism on the Eve of the Millennium* (Reno: University of Nevada Press, 2000); Kemal Kirisci and Gareth M. Winrow, *The Kurdish Question and Turkey: An Example of Trans-State Ethnic Conflict* (London: Frank Cass, 1997).

14. Aleksandar Pavkovic, *The Fragmentation of Yugoslavia: Nationalism and War in the Balkans* (Hampshire, U.K.: Palgrave Macmillan, 2000); Dusan Kecmanovic, *Ethnic Times: Exploring Ethnonationalism in the Former Yugoslavia* (Westport, Conn.: Praeger, 2001).

15. Rawi Abdelal, *National Purpose in the World Economy: Post-Soviet States in Comparative Perspective* (Ithaca, N.Y.: Cornell University Press, 2001).

Part One

THEORIES OF NATIONALISM

Chapter One

Mainstream Theories of the Nation and Nationalism

Conventional social theories on the nature and sources of nationalism and ethnic conflict cover a time span extending from classical to contemporary theoretical statements that provide a conservative perspective to the analyses of nationalism and ethnonational phenomena that have taken center stage in the late-twentieth and early-twenty-first centuries. Mainstream theories of the nation and nationalism have played an important role in rationalizing the nationalist agenda by providing functionalist lenses through which the phenomenon of nationalism can be studied much as religion, values, and culture in the idealist tradition.

This chapter provides an overview of the most influential classical and contemporary bourgeois theories of nationalism and ethnic conflict that came to dominate the mainstream literature in the late-nineteenth and twentieth centuries. While the analysis presented provides an outline of several strands of bourgeois theorizing on the nation and nationalism, no attempt is made here to undertake a comprehensive and exhaustive survey of all mainstream bourgeois theories of nationalism and ethnic conflict. Instead, I present here the highlights of some of the more prominent conventional theories on this question as a background to an in-depth critique of these theories throughout the remainder of this chapter.

CLASSICAL MAINSTREAM STATEMENTS ON THE NATION AND NATIONALISM

The central figures that have occupied a prominent place in the literature on classical bourgeois theories of the nation and nationalism have been Ernest

Renan and Max Weber. There are, of course, other influential theorists who have made a lasting contribution to the development of mainstream, conventional theories of nationalism and national/ethnic identity, including Jean-Jacques Rousseau, Johann Herder, Johann Fichte, and Giuseppi Mazzini, among others.[1] However, Renan's and Weber's classical statements on these phenomena stand out as prime examples of bourgeois theories that have informed, in one way or another, all other subsequent mainstream formulations of the nation, nationalism, and ethnonational conflict in the twentieth century.

In his classic statement *"Qu'est-ce qu'une nation?"* originally delivered as a lecture at the Sorbonne in 1882, Ernest Renan provides the following definition of the nation:

> A nation is a soul, a spiritual principle. Only two things, actually, constitute this soul, this spiritual principle. One is in the past, the other is in the present. One is the possession in common of a rich legacy of remembrances; the other is the actual consent, the desire to live together, the will to continue to value the heritage which all hold in common. . . . To have common glories in the past, a common will in the present; to have accomplished great things together, to wish to do so again, that is the essential condition for being a nation.[2]

"A nation," Renan continues, "is a grand solidarity constituted by the sentiment of sacrifices which one has made and those that one is disposed to make again."[3] Thus, according to Renan's view,

> A great aggregation of men, with a healthy spirit and warmth of heart, creates a moral conscience which is called a nation. When this moral conscience proves its strength by sacrifices that demand abdication of the individual for the benefit of the community, it is legitimate, and it has a right to exist.[4]

This subjective, idealist view of the nation is consistent with Renan's conclusion, where he states:

> Through their varied, frequently opposing, abilities, nations serve the common cause of civilization; each holds one note in the concert of humanity, which, in the long run, is the highest ideal to which we can aspire.[5]

Defining the nation in these terms, Renan highlights one aspect of the fundamental features of mainstream, bourgeois theories of the nation and nationalism: a subjective, idealist conception of the nation that is largely a product of the mind, an abstraction that emerges from the collective imagination. Another, equally important, aspect of bourgeois theorizing on this question is the overemphasis on ethnic and cultural phenomena to explain the origins and development of the nation and nationalism. In this view, culture and ethnicity, divorced from class forces in society, take on a life of their own and form the basis of social relations and social movements and their ideologies, including nationalism.

Max Weber's classic statement on this question fits into both of these ideological frames of thought. A subjective, idealist conception of the nation that incorporates an ethnocultural definition of nationalism and national identity is how Weber developed his approach to this question in the classic context. In a key passage in one of his major works, Weber writes:

> If the concept of "nation" can in any way be defined unambiguously, it certainly cannot be stated in terms of empirical qualities common to those who count as members of the nation. In the sense of those using the term at a given time, the concept undoubtedly means, above all, that one may exact from certain groups of men a specific sentiment of solidarity in the face of other groups. Thus, the concept belongs in the sphere of values.[6]

In this sense, "A nation is a community of sentiment," writes Weber. "And one must be clearly aware of the fact that sentiments of solidarity, very heterogeneous in both their nature and their origin, are comprised within national sentiments."[7] Moreover:

> the idea of the "nation" is apt to include the notions of common descent and of an essential, though frequently indefinite, homogeneity. The nation has these notions in common with the sentiment of solidarity of ethnic communities, which is also nourished from various sources.[8]

Weber goes on to point out that the "sentiment of solidarity" that goes with the "idea of the nation" is well integrated into a cultural frame of reference facilitated by a collective "mission" that solidifies a community and gives it its sociocultural, as well as national, identity:

> The earliest and most energetic manifestations of the idea [of the nation], in some form, even though it may have been veiled, have contained the legend of a providential "mission." Those to whom the representatives of the idea zealously turned were expected to shoulder this mission. Another element of the early idea was the notion that this mission was facilitated solely through the very cultivation of the peculiarity of the group set off as a nation. Therewith, in so far as its self-justification is sought in the value of its content, this mission can consistently be thought of only as a specific "culture" mission. The significance of the "nation" is usually anchored in the superiority, or at least the irreplaceability, of the culture values that are to be preserved and developed only through the cultivation of the peculiarity of the group.[9]

Weber's conventional, idealist views on the nation and national identity in such cultural, value-centered terms complements well the arguments of other classical mainstream theorists, such as Renan, who have provided the foundations for subsequent bourgeois theories of the nation and nationalism developed by their contemporaries.

Among later bourgeois theorists who have followed this path, one may include Hans Kohn, Carlton Hayes, and Louis Snyder. In his book *The Idea of Nationalism*, Hans Kohn writes, "Nationalism is first and foremost a state of mind, an act of consciousness."[10] Kohn goes on to state, "Nationalism is an idea, an idée-force, which fills man's brain and heart with new thoughts and new sentiments, and drives him to translate his consciousness into deeds of organized action."[11]

"Nationalism," writes Kohn, "recognizes the nation-state as the ideal form of political organization."[12] Hence, in this sense, "Nationalism demands the nation-state; the creation of the nation-state strengthens nationalism."[13] Elsewhere, in *Nationalism: Its Meaning and History*, Kohn writes, "Nationalism is a state of mind, in which the supreme loyalty of the individual is felt to be due the nation-state."[14]

The relationship between nationality and the nation-state is an aspect of the phenomenon of nationalism that Carlton Hayes also emphasized in his writings on nationalism. For Hayes, the term *nationalism* is used in the first instance "to denote an actual historical process, the process of establishing nationalities as political units, of building out of tribes and empires the modern institution of the national state."[15] On the other hand, nationalism, according to Hayes, can also be described as "a contemporary popular belief, the belief that one's own nationality or national state has such intrinsic worth and excellence as to require one to be loyal to it above every other thing and particularly to bestow upon it what amounts to supreme religious worship."[16] Thus, in this latter sense, nationalism is described by Hayes as a phenomenon that has metaphysical properties. Viewing nationalism as a belief (as a religion), Hayes, in his book *Nationalism: A Religion*, goes on to characterize the phenomenon in broad moralistic terms—as a force for "good" or as a force for "evil," that is, "as a blessing or as a curse," as he puts it.[17]

Louis Snyder, another mainstream theorist in the tradition of Kohn and Hayes, provides a similar view on the nature and meaning of modern nationalism.[18] Attempting to define nationalism at the broadest and most general level, Snyder writes, "The term nationalism admits of no simple definition. It is a complex phenomenon, often vague and mysterious in character."[19] Speaking of "its most perplexing feature," he says, nationalism "may differ in its forms" as it is "used in so many different senses" and "has many faces," such that "the effort continue as scholars seek to unravel the mysteries of an elusive historical phenomenon."[20]

Having mystified the phenomenon beyond any concrete social meaning, Snyder defines nationalism as a "state of mind" as Kohn had done, as nationalism "is a condition of mind, feeling, or sentiment."[21] "Nationalism is a powerful emotion," Snyder writes, "a form of consciousness by which the individual proclaims his supreme loyalty to the nation."[22]

This broad, psychological and metaphysical focus on the purported "mysterious" and "elusive" nature of nationalism by these earlier mainstream theorists has given way to a variety of more recent contemporary bourgeois theories that are more sophisticated in their reasoning through the adoption of a sociocultural perspective that incorporates questions related to ethnicity and ethnonational issues. Although these later theorists have, as those before them, remained silent on class and the class nature of nationalism and ethnonational conflict, they have nonetheless provided divergent perspectives that require our attention at least briefly.

CONTEMPORARY MAINSTREAM VIEWS
ON THE NATION AND NATIONALISM

Among the most prominent of contemporary mainstream bourgeois theorists of nationalism one could cite Elie Kedourie, Ernest Gellner, Walker Connor, Karl Deutsch, John Breuilly, and Anthony D. Smith.[23] We shall focus here on the views of three of these theorists—Kedourie, Gellner, and Connor—as representing a sampling of dominant mainstream views on this question in recent years.

Elie Kedourie, one of the most prominent, if not the most prominent, of more recent contemporary mainstream theorists of nationalism, provides a critique of various theories of the nation and nationalism that base their legitimacy on one or another aspect of social and historical existence. "In nationalist doctrine," he writes, "language, race, culture, and sometimes even religion, constitute different aspects of the same primordial entity, the nation."[24] While "it is misplaced ingenuity," Kedourie continues, "to try and classify nationalisms according to the particular aspect which they choose to emphasize," the premises on which such theory is based make its claims all the more evident:

What is beyond doubt is that the doctrine divides humanity into separate and distinct nations, claims that such nations must constitute sovereign states, and asserts that the members of a nation reach freedom and fulfillment by cultivating the peculiar identity of their own nation and by sinking their own persons in the greater whole of the nation.[25]

To Kedourie, such a view that characterizes the nation and the division of the world by nation-states as natural, that is, as part of the natural order of things, is unfounded and is therefore a fallacy:

> The inventors of the doctrine tried to prove that nations are obvious and natural divisions of the human race, by appealing to history, anthropology, and linguistics. But the attempt breaks down since, whatever ethnological or philological doctrine may be fashionable for the moment, there is no convincing reason why the fact that people speak the same language or belong to the same race should, by itself, entitle them to enjoy a government exclusively their own.[26]

Rejecting materialist approaches to the problem, Kedourie opts for an idealist definition of the nation and nationalism based on Ernest Renan's classic statement on the individual will. Referring to Renan's view of the nation, Kedourie approvingly writes, "Having examined the different criteria which are used to distinguish nations, and having found them wanting, [Renan] concluded that the will of the individual must ultimately indicate whether a nation exists or not."[27] Kedourie goes on to argue that the individual, "in pursuit of self-determination, wills himself as the member of a nation."[28] In agreement with Renan's own description of the nation as "a daily plebiscite," Kedourie points out that "the metaphor is felicitous, if only because it indicates so well that nationalism is ultimately based on will." Thus, Kedourie continues, "National self-determination is, in the final analysis, a determination of the will; and nationalism is, in the first place, a method of teaching the right determination of the will."[29]

Such a subjectivist argument, divorced from the social basis that gives rise to the phenomenon of nationalism in the form of a collective national will, is a product of an idealist formulation and lacks a basis in material reality. Failure to identify the social and class forces that are the decisive agents of nationalist ideology and nationalist movements leads Kedourie to a blind alley and an intellectual eclecticism that contributes very little to our understanding of this important social phenomenon.

Ernest Gellner, another prominent mainstream bourgeois theorist of nationalism, provides a different set of answers to this question. For Gellner, the primary unifying factor that nationalism utilizes to rally the masses behind the nationalist banner is culture. Culture, in Gellner's view, plays a decisive role in defining national identity, and the particular use to which culture is put by the nationalist forces determines the impact of nationalism on society: "nationalism, which sometimes takes pre-existing cultures and turns them into nations, sometimes invents them, and often obliterates pre-existing cultures."[30]

In a fashion similar to that of Kedourie's idealist, subjectivist argument, Gellner argues that "it is nationalism which engenders nations, and not the other way round."[31] "Admittedly," he concedes, "nationalism uses the pre-existing, historically inherited proliferation of cultures or cultural wealth, though it uses them very selectively, and it most often transforms them radically."[32] But, Gellner points out:

> The great, but valid, paradox is this: nations can be defined only in terms of the age of nationalism, rather than, as you might expect, the other way round. It is not the case that the "age of nationalism" is a mere summation of the awakening and political self-assertion of this, that, or the other nation. Rather, when general social conditions make for standardized, homogeneous, centrally sustained high cultures, pervading entire populations and not just elite minorities, a situation arises in which well-defined educationally sanctioned and unified cultures constitute very nearly the only kind of unit with which men willingly and often ardently identify. The cultures now seem to be the natural repositories of political legitimacy.[33]

Elsewhere, in his more recent book, *Encounters with Nationalism*, Gellner writes:

> Modern nationalism, which is a passionate identification with large, anonymous communities of shared culture and cultural imagery, creates its units out of pre-existing differences of various kinds. Among these, religious ones are important (irrespective of whether the faith which defined the religions in question is still upheld).[34]

"It is this new importance of a shared culture," Gellner asserts, "which makes men into nationalists":

> The congruence between their own culture and that of the political, economic and educational bureaucracies which surround them, becomes the most important single fact of their lives. They must be concerned with that congruence, with its achievement or its protection: and this turns them into nationalists. Their first political concern must be that they are members of a political unit which identifies with *their* idiom, ensures its perpetuation, employment, defence. That is what nationalism is.[35]

Thus, "In the past," Gellner concludes, "social structure not culture held society together; but that has now changed. *That* is the secret of nationalism: the new role of culture in industrial and industrialized society."[36]

Notwithstanding some basic philosophical differences, Gellner's emphasis on culture as the source of nationalism and ethnonational identity (i.e., his emphasis on the primacy of superstructural phenomena) nevertheless places him in the same ideological camp as Kedourie. Thus, while Kedourie sees nationalism as an idea and speaks of the individual will and Gellner bases his argument on cultural factors, both their theories are constructed in the super-structural sphere, that is, in the realm of ideas, values, beliefs, tradition, culture—not in the sphere of fundamental social-structural conditions, let alone class and class relations.

Walker Connor is another contemporary mainstream bourgeois theorist who has had a major impact on dominant mainstream theories of the nation and nationalism.[37] Viewing the nation in similarly psychological terms as associated with belief systems, Connor provides the following observation:

> Defining and conceptualizing the nation is . . . difficult because the essence of a nation is intangible. This essence is a psychological bond that joins a people and differentiates it, in the subconscious conviction of its members, from all other people in a most vital way. The nature of that bond and its well-spring remain shadowy and elusive, and the consequent difficulty of defining the nation is usually acknowledged by those who attempt this task.[38]

Connor goes on to emphasize that "when analyzing sociopolitical situations, what ultimately matters is not *what is* but *what people believe is*. And a subconscious belief in the group's separate origin and evolution is an important ingredient of national psychology."[39] Thus, referring to "a mass psychological vibration predicated upon an intuitive sense of consanguinity," Connor places national identity and nationalism in the sphere of beliefs and feelings and writes, "It is the intuitive conviction which can give to nations a psychological dimension."[40]

Aside from the similarly idealist philosophical and theoretical orientations of these contemporary mainstream bourgeois theorists, the thread that runs through their ideologically tainted conservative arguments is their open and undisguised anticommunism. It is, in essence, their uniform politically charged ideological attack on Marxism that unites these bourgeois apologists to develop their respective anti-Marxist (bourgeois) theories to counter the claims of the Marxist classics. That this is the case with bourgeois theories of nationalism in general, and with the two of the more prominent contemporary bourgeois theorists like Kedourie and Gellner in particular, is made clear by their own pronouncements in no uncertain terms.

Elie Kedourie, for example, in the July 1984 dated "Afterword" to the fourth, expanded edition of his book *Nationalism*, published posthumously in 1993, writes:

> Marxism has also purported to offer an explanation of nationalism which makes it into an epiphenomenon which appears at a particular stage of economic development, when the bourgeoisie and its capitalist mode of production are in the ascendant. Nationalism is an expression of bourgeois interests. Here too, what

nationalist ideology asserts or denies becomes of no interest, since it is a product of false consciousness, which must fade away as capitalism inevitably succumbs to its crisis. The bourgeoisie will then be dispossessed and swept away by the victorious proletariat, and with it all the superstructure of the bourgeois state, bourgeois culture, bourgeois ideology, etc. This is a manifest absurdity, since all the evidence shows that nationalism is not a "reflection" of the capitalist mode of production, and that it can occur in societies which have the most varied social and economic structures. Marxists, of course, have come to see this and have ingeniously tried to accommodate nationalism within the Marxist scheme in a manner such as to avoid absurd and impossible conclusions. But these efforts have, not surprisingly, failed to carry conviction, since Marxism is impotent to break loose from the regimentation imposed by its founder's crude categories.[41]

In the "Introduction to the Fourth Edition" of *Nationalism*, dated Spring 1992, written only weeks before his death in June of that year, Kedourie refers to "the implosion and self-destruction of Bolshevik and other Socialist regimes" and writes, "The disintegration and failure of socialism in the Soviet empire and its satellites has not meant the disappearance of the ideological style of politics—far from it. As we can see it has produced, in a revulsion against socialist tyranny, a revival or recrudescence of nationalism."[42] Contrasting the historic rise of nationalism in Europe in the previous century, Kedourie attacks socialism as its rival in no uncertain terms when he writes:

> The other powerful ideology which purported to provide a remedy for human alienation and unhappiness was socialism. The cause of these ills, as socialism diagnosed it, was private property. The first man who fenced in his property, as Rousseau argued, brought unfreedom into the world, and human beings will not taste freedom alike from oppression and self-alienation until private property is abolished. This other ideological obsession has in its turn been tested to destruction in twentieth-century politics. Like nationalism it has produced not happiness or spiritual fulfillment, or even material prosperity, but, on the contrary, unparalleled oppression and misery, and it has sunk by the weight of its own misconceived ideals.[43]

Ernest Gellner goes a step further in attacking Marxism in his latest politically motivated, ideological polemic designed to discredit an intellectual orientation of long standing. In his most recent book, *Encounters with Nationalism*, published in 1994, Gellner writes:

> The Marxist mistakes in social metaphysics and in sociology converge on what of course is the single most crucial and disastrous error in the system. The supposition that the communist social order will require no political organization but will in some unexplained way be self-adjusting. . . . The sad consequence is

that societies living "under the banner of Marxism" are simply deprived of any idiom in which even to discuss their political predicament. . . . As for the political form of communist society, they cannot really discuss it at all.[44]

Gellner continues with his politically charged diatribe to score a few reactionary points for his conservative bourgeois colleagues, when he writes:

It is indeed true that Marxism is formally the official doctrine and state religion over extensive parts of the globe. However, at present neither rulers nor subjects in these states have much faith in it, or take it very seriously. It is exceedingly hard to find Marxists in Marxist societies, though it is still possible to find some in non-Marxist ones.[45]

Finally, Gellner cannot resist taking pleasure in the recent transformations in the former Soviet Union and East European socialist states, when he writes with a contemptuous sarcasm that makes a mockery of the pursuit of scientific knowledge and scholarship. "Marxism," he says, "had taught that civil society was a kind of moral fraud, but 70 years of secular messianism has engendered a passionate thirst for just this fraud":

Marxism had seen the liberal state as a kind of executive committee of the bourgeoisie; now a committee is striving, not too convincingly, to create a bourgeoisie which it could serve, and hopes that it is not too blatant a lumpenbourgeoisie. We can only watch these efforts with trepidation, and wish them well. The best one can say is that a dogmatic pessimism is unjustified.[46]

There are, of course, other more sophisticated and sociologically oriented bourgeois theories that focus on ethnic groups and ethnonationalist movements as central to the nationalist project placed in historical context, such as those developed by Anthony D. Smith, Charles Tilly, Michael Hechter, and Anthony Giddens.[47] Still, in one form or another, these "liberal" attempts to explain the origin, nature, and development of nations and nationalism, as well as ethnicity and ethnonational conflict, are predicated on a variety of anti-Marxist contemporary mainstream perspectives that have become quite fashionable in bourgeois circles in recent years, as in the case of Giddens's neo-Weberian critique of Marxism in his book *A Contemporary Critique of Historical Materialism*, where he attacks Marxists, and Marxism in general, for failing to provide the "right" answers.[48]

While Giddens asserts on page 1 of his book, "My intention is not to produce a critique of historical materialism written in hostile mien, declaring Marxism to be redundant or exhausted," a few sentences later he unleashes an all-out attack against Marxism in an attempt to accomplish precisely the opposite of what he claims. There "is much in Marx that is mistaken, ambiguous or inconsistent," he writes, "and in many respects Marx's writings exemplify features of nineteenth-century thought which are plainly defective."[49]

"Let me try to put the facts of the matter as bluntly as possible," Giddens continues:

> If by "historical materialism" we mean the conception that the history of human societies can be understood in terms of the progressive augmentation of the forces of production, then it is based on false premises, and the time has come finally to abandon it. If historical materialism means that "the history of all hitherto existing society is the history of class struggles," it is so patently erroneous that it is difficult to see why so many have felt obliged to take it seriously. If, finally, historical materialism means that Marx's scheme of the evolution of societies (from tribal society, Ancient society, feudalism, to capitalism; and thence to socialism, together with the "stagnant" offshoot of the "Asiatic Mode of Production" in the East) provides a defensible basis for analysing world history, then it is also to be rejected.[50]

"First of all," Giddens admits, "much of this book is an attack upon the idea of 'mode of production' as a useful analytical concept."[51] "Anyone who rejects Marx's evolutionary scheme, and a good deal of the substantive content of his materialist conception of history besides—as I do—" Giddens continues, "must pursue the implications right through."[52] Thus, "Marx's more general pronouncements upon human history, especially in those most famous of all passages, in the 'Preface' to *A Contribution to the Critique of Political Economy*, have to be treated with great caution and, in some major respects, simply discarded."[53] Finally, "Marx's comments on non-Capitalist societies," Giddens writes, "are relatively scrappy and often unoriginal. Some of them, in my view, are just as erroneous as are certain of his more general statements. It is not their unsatisfactory character but rather the tenacity with which many Marxists have sought to cling to whatever gems they claim to find there which is astonishing."[54]

Following his sweeping attack on Marx, Giddens offers the following proposal: "In diverging from Marx I want to propose the elements of an alternative interpretation of history."[55] He writes:

> A fundamental component of my arguments is the supposition that the articulation of time-space relations in social systems has to be examined in conjunction with the generation of *power*. A preoccupation with power forms a leading thread of this book. I maintain that power was never satisfactorily theorized by Marx, and that this failure is at origin of some of the chief limitations of his scheme of historical analysis.[56]

This is a claim that is totally unfounded, as power and power relations constitute the cornerstone of Marx's analysis of society and social relations. As to Giddens's critique of Marxist views on nationalism, he offers the same worn-out anticommunist fallacies: "Even the most orthodox of Marxists," he writes, "are today prepared to concede that there is little to be found in Marx's writings relevant to the interpretation of the rise of nationalism."[57] Elsewhere, in the second volume of his book, Giddens continues:

> It is manifestly the case that Marx paid little attention to the nature and impact of nationalism, and the comments he does make are mostly neither instructive nor profound. Subsequent Marxists have been very much concerned with "the national question," but it cannot be pretended that the literature thereby generated has done a great deal to illuminate the nature or origins of nationalism. None of the various Marxist interpretations which seek to treat nationalism as some kind of masked expression of the interests of the dominant class has much plausibility either.[58]

Finally, a more recent and widely adopted strand of bourgeois theorizing on nationalism and national identity has been the idea of citizenship and identity politics. Here, one finds a series of arguments advanced by Charles Tilly, Rogers Brubaker, Michael Hecter, Liah Greenfeld, and others who attempt to link nationhood and identity to citizenship and democratic governance to situate the individual within the context of community and communal life both at the local and broader national levels.

"Citizenship and nationhood are intensely contested issues," writes Rogers Brubaker, and "they are likely to remain so for the foreseeable future."[59] "As a powerful instrument of social closure," Brubaker continues, "citizenship occupies a central place in the administrative structure and political culture of the modern nation-state and state system."[60] Moreover,

> Citizenship is not only an instrument of closure, a prerequisite for the enjoyment of certain rights, or for participation in certain types of interaction. It is also an object of closure, a status to which access is restricted. From a global perspective, to be sure, citizenship is virtually universal. In this perspective, citizenship is an international filing system, a mechanism for allocating persons to states.[61]

Charles Tilly, in his book *Citizenship, Identity, and Social History*, asserts that "no standard definition of citizenship has yet gained scholarly consensus."[62] He goes on to argue, however, "Today's dissensus gives us no reason to abandon the search for a useful definition."[63]

> For theoretical and historical clarity, we should confine the definition of citizenship to a certain kind of tie: *a continuing series of transactions between persons and agents of a given state in which each has enforceable rights and obligations uniquely by virtue of (1) the person's membership in an exclusive*

category, the native-born plus the naturalized and (2) the agent's relation to the state rather than any other authority the agent may enjoy. Citizenship thus forms a special sort of contract.[64]

"As a category," Tilly continues:

Citizenship designates a set of actors–citizens—distinguished by their shared privileged position vis-à-vis some particular state. As a tie, citizenship identifies an enforceable mutual relation between an actor and state agents. As a role, citizenship includes all of an actor's relations to others that depend on the actor's relation to a particular state. And as an identity, citizenship can refer to the experience and public representation of category, tie or role.[65]

Besides its seemingly functionalist approach to the subject matter, this line of argument is characteristic of the entire group of theorists who link citizenship and identity to nationhood and nationalism.[66] Common to all of their theories is the lack of an analysis of the class nature of nationalism and citizenship. As such, the arguments made by citizenship theorists remain in the realm of abstract and universalist "ideal-typical" models of society and social relations. As Tilly admits, "The definition [of citizenship] is, of course, ideal-typical, abstracting from particular ties connecting this citizen with that agent."[67] Thus, as is the case with other variants of classical and contemporary mainstream theories of nationalism, theories of citizenship and identity politics likewise suffer from the effects of bourgeois idealism.

In all the cases discussed above, including both earlier and recent mainstream efforts to search for alternative non-Marxist theories of nation, national identity, nationalism, and ethnonational conflict, the underlying driving force of bourgeois theorizing on these questions has been a rejection of class analysis in favor of bourgeois eclecticism, which, in essence, reveals the anti-Marxist nature of bourgeois "scholarship" that is presented as the only acceptable and viable alternative that supposedly transcends Marxism.

In the next chapter, I sweep aside such diversionary, eclectic, bourgeois-idealist attempts at sowing confusion on this important subject, and provide the outlines of an alternative Marxist (i.e., dialectical and historical materialist) theory that is firmly based on a class analysis of national phenomena that reveals the class nature of nationalism and ethnic conflict to expose the class forces involved in promoting and perpetuating class-driven national interests that have fostered, and continue to foster, ethnonational conflict so as to derail or postpone class struggle and social revolution.

NOTES

1. The term *nationalism* first appeared in classical literature in 1774 in a text written by Johann Herder. See Peter Alter, *Nationalism* (London: Edward Arnold, 1989). John Hutchinson and Anthony D. Smith in the "Introduction" to their edited book *Nationalism* ([New York: Oxford University Press, 1994], p. 5) point out that "as an ideology and discourse, nationalism became prevalent in North America and Western Europe in the latter half of the eighteenth century. . . . The dates that are often singled out as signaling the advent of nationalism include 1775 (the First Partition of Poland), 1776 (the American Declaration of Independence), 1789 and 1792 (the commencement and second phase of the French Revolution), and 1807 (Fichte's *Addresses to the German Nation*)."

2. Ernest Renan, *"Qu'est-ce qu'une nation?"* excerpted in Hutchinson and Smith, *Nationalism*, p. 17.

3. Renan, *"Qu'est-ce qu'une nation?"* p. 17.

4. Renan, *"Qu'est-ce qu'une nation?"* p. 18.

5. Renan, *"Qu'est-ce qu'une nation?"* p. 18.

6. Max Weber, *From Max Weber: Essays in Sociology*, edited by H. H. Gerth and C. Wright Mills (New York: Oxford University Press, 1946), p. 172.

7. Weber, *From Max Weber*, p. 179.

8. Weber, *From Max Weber*, p. 173.

9. Weber, *From Max Weber*, p. 176.

10. Hans Kohn, *The Idea of Nationalism* (New York: Collier Books, 1944), p. 10.

11. Kohn, *Idea of Nationalism*, p. 19.

12. Kohn, *Idea of Nationalism*, p. 16.

13. Kohn, *Idea of Nationalism*, p. 19.

14. Hans Kohn, *Nationalism: Its Meaning and History* (Princeton, N.J.: Van Nostrand, 1965), p. 9.

15. Carlton J. H. Hayes, *Essays on Nationalism* (New York: Macmillan, 1937), p. 245.

16. Hayes, *Essays on Nationalism*, p. 245.

17. Carlton J. H. Hayes, *Nationalism: A Religion* (New York: Macmillan, 1960).

18. Louis L. Snyder, *The Meaning of Nationalism* (New Brunswick, N.J.: Rutgers University Press, 1954).

19. Louis L. Snyder, *Encyclopedia of Nationalism* (New York: Paragon House, 1990), p. 245.

20. Snyder, *Encyclopedia of Nationalism*, p. 245.

21. Louis L. Snyder, ed., *The Dynamics of Nationalism* (Princeton, N.J.: Van Nostrand, 1964), p. 2.

22. Snyder, *The Meaning of Nationalism*, pp. 74–75.

23. See, for example: Elie Kedourie, *Nationalism*, 4th ed. (Malden, Mass.: Blackwell, 1993, first published in 1960); Ernest Gellner, *Nations and Nationalism* (Ithaca, N.Y.: Cornell University Press, 1983) and *Encounters with Nationalism* (Malden, Mass.: Blackwell, 1994); Walker Connor, "A Nation Is a Nation, Is a State, Is an Ethnic Group Is a . . . " *Ethnic and Racial Studies* 1, no. 4 (October 1978) and *Ethnona-*

tionalism: The Quest for Understanding (Princeton, N.J.: Princeton University Press, 1994); Karl Deutsch, *Nationalism and Social Communication* (Cambridge, Mass.: MIT Press, 1953); John Breuilly, *Nationalism and the State*, 2nd ed. (Chicago: University of Chicago Press, 1994); Anthony D. Smith, *Theories of Nationalism*, 2nd ed. (New York: Holms and Meier Publishers, 1983) and Anthony D. Smith, *The Ethnic Revival* (New York: Cambridge University Press, 1981); John Hutchinson and Anthony D. Smith, eds., *Nationalism* (New York: Oxford University Press, 1994).

24. Kedourie, *Nationalism*, p. 67.

25. Kedourie, *Nationalism*, p. 67.

26. Kedourie, *Nationalism*, p. 74.

27. Kedourie, *Nationalism*, p. 75.

28. Kedourie, *Nationalism*, p. 75.

29. Kedourie, *Nationalism*, p. 76.

30. Gellner, *Nations and Nationalism*, p. 49.

31. Gellner, *Nations and Nationalism*, p. 55.

32. Gellner, *Nations and Nationalism*, p. 55.

33. Gellner, *Nations and Nationalism*, p. 55.

34. Gellner, *Encounters with Nationalism*, p. 178.

35. Gellner, *Encounters with Nationalism*, p. viii, emphasis in the original.

36. Gellner, *Encounters with Nationalism*, p. 63.

37. See Daniele Conversi, *Ethnonationalism in the Contemporary World: Walker Connor and the Study of Nationalism* (New York: Routledge, 2002).

38. Connor, "A Nation Is a Nation," p. 379.

39. Connor, "A Nation Is a Nation," p. 380.

40. Connor, "A Nation Is a Nation," p. 381.

41. Kedourie, *Nationalism*, pp. 141–42.

42. Kedourie, *Nationalism*, p. xvii.

43. Kedourie, *Nationalism*, p. xvi.

44. Gellner, *Encounters with Nationalism*, pp. 6–7.

45. Gellner, *Encounters with Nationalism*, p. 64.

46. Gellner, *Encounters with Nationalism*, p. 179.

47. See Anthony D. Smith, *The Ethnic Origins of Nations* (Oxford, U.K.: Blackwell, 1986) and Anthony D. Smith, *The Nation in History: Historiographical Debates about Ethnicity and Nationalism* (Hanover, N.H.: University Press of New England, 2000); Charles Tilly, *The Politics of Collective Violence* (Cambridge, U.K.: Cambridge University Press, 2003); Michael Hechter, *Containing Nationalism* (New York: Oxford University Press, 2000); and Anthony Giddens, *A Contemporary Critique of Historical Materialism* (Berkeley: University of California Press, 1981).

48. Giddens, *A Contemporary Critique of Historical Materialism*.

49. Giddens, *A Contemporary Critique of Historical Materialism*, p. 1.

50. Giddens, *A Contemporary Critique of Historical Materialism*, pp. 1–2.

51. Giddens, *A Contemporary Critique of Historical Materialism*, p. 7.

52. Giddens, *A Contemporary Critique of Historical Materialism*, p. 24.

53. Giddens, *A Contemporary Critique of Historical Materialism*, p. 2.

54. Giddens, *A Contemporary Critique of Historical Materialism*, pp. 2–3.

55. Giddens, *A Contemporary Critique of Historical Materialism*, p. 3.

56. Giddens, *A Contemporary Critique of Historical Materialism*.

57. Giddens, *A Contemporary Critique of Historical Materialism*, p. 11.

58. Anthony Giddens, *The Nation-State and Violence* (Berkeley: University of California Press, 1985), pp. 212–13.

59. Rogers Brubaker, *Citizenship and Nationhood in France and Germany* (Cambridge, Mass.: Harvard University Press, 1992), p. 189.

60. Brubaker, *Citizenship and Nationhood in France and Germany*, p. 23.

61. Brubaker, *Citizenship and Nationhood in France and Germany*, p. 32.

62. Charles Tilly, ed., *Citizenship, Identity, and Social History* (Cambridge, U.K.: Cambridge University Press, 1995), p. 8.

63. Tilly, *Citizenship, Identity, and Social History*, p. 8.

64. Tilly, *Citizenship, Identity, and Social History*. Italics in the original, p. 8.

65. Tilly, *Citizenship, Identity, and Social History*, p. 8.

66. See T. K. Oommen, ed., *Citizenship and National Identity* (New Delhi: Sage, 1997).

67. Tilly, *Citizenship, Identity, and Social History*, p. 8.

Chapter Two

Toward a Marxist Theory of Nationalism

This chapter attempts to develop an alternative Marxist theory of nationalism based on the principles of historical materialism. Going beyond the surface phenomena of national, religious, and ethnic conflicts that mainstream social scientists have studied as determinants of social relations, this chapter provides a class analysis of the nature and dynamics of conflicts along national, religious, and ethnic lines and attempts to develop an alternative theory that explains the root causes of such phenomena in class terms.

THE CRITIQUE FROM WITHIN: CRITICS OF MARXISM ON NATIONALISM AND THE NATIONAL QUESTION

As we pointed out in the previous chapter, mainstream bourgeois theorists and commentators have criticized Marxism for failing to come to terms with nationalism and the national question, and for underestimating its potent force in effecting change. Bourgeois critics, in their zeal to undermine and discredit Marxism as a viable theory of society and social relations, have attempted time and again to undermine the legitimacy of Marxist social scientific inquiry as part of a sustained attack on Marxism throughout the cold war years. A major ingredient of this anticommunist assault on Marxist theory during this period has been a concerted effort to refute the primacy of class— the central concept that informs the Marxist analysis of society and social relations.

This bourgeois, conservative criticism of Marxism, which has a long history stretching back more than a century, is not surprising, nor unexpected, as it conforms to long-held views that have always been hostile to Marxism.

What is disturbing and troublesome, however, is that this same kind of criticism of Marxism is also leveled by some self-styled "Marxists" who have contributed to the anticommunist intellectual crusade aimed at discrediting Marxism for its "failure" to address the complex issues surrounding nationalism and the national question, coupled with charges of class reductionism. Here one can include Tom Nairn, Benedict Anderson, Ernesto Laclau, Ephraim Nimni, Horace B. Davis, and Eric Hobsbawm, among others. What is common to all these critics from within Marxism (and here is where their positions coincide with that of their conservative bourgeois counterparts) is their subjective, idealist conception of nationalism informed by an ethnocultural analysis devoid of class.

Tom Nairn, in his book *The Break-Up of Britain*, for example, claims that: "The theory of nationalism represents Marxism's great historical failure."[1] Adding to the list of "failures," where he cites, "Marxism's shortcomings over imperialism, the state, the falling rate of profit and the immiseration of the masses are certainly old battlefields," Nairn writes, "Yet none of these is as important, as fundamental, as the problem of nationalism, either in theory or in political practice."[2] To correct this situation, he offers the following insight: nationalism is an autonomous, ideological force that is based on an idea; it is an irrational response to general frustration.

Taking this critique a step further, Benedict Anderson, in his book *Imagined Communities*, asserts, "Nationalism has proved an uncomfortable *anomaly* for Marxist theory and, precisely for that reason, has been largely elided, rather than confronted."[3] And what is this great discovery that Marxists have failed to confront? The discovery that the nation is an imagined cultural community and nationalism is a product of the collective imagination that is as real as religion and cosmology!

Ernesto Laclau, in a recent commentary on Marxism and the national question that echoes Nairn's and Anderson's critique, boldly states, "Blindness to the national factor has been recurrent in the history of Marxism right from the beginning. These limitations are to be found even in the highest moments of Marxist theorisation on the national question."[4] Yet, Laclau is unable to offer a vision other than old, worn-out bourgeois rationalizations on the irrationality of nationalism that is as ideologically blind as he alleges Marxist theorizing to be. Saturated with idealist conceptions emerging from abstract reasoning, nationalism to Laclau is no more real than those who believe it to be.

Ephraim Nimni, who credits Laclau's work as having had a "profound influence" on his intellectual development, goes even further in his recent book *Marxism and Nationalism* in attacking Marxists for their "insensitivity" toward the "uniqueness of nationalist ideologies" and say, "The national question did not disappear because Marxists wished it to do so."[5] Stemming from this criticism is Nimni's attack on Marxism for its alleged "economic reductionism"—by which he means various aspects of superstructural phenomena are reflections of the economic base as "all meaningful changes within the social arena take place in the sphere of economic (class) relations" and that "economic relations of production are the unique source of causality."[6] Associated with this position is his indictment of Marxism for its "class reductionism":

> A class reductionist approach represents an important shift of emphasis within the same conceptual framework. Social classes are considered the only possible historical subjects so that ideologies and other superstructural phenomena (such as nationalism and the national arena in general) "belong" to the paradigmatic area of influence of class position. . . . Political and other activities may advance or delay (according to the circumstances) the outcome of the relations between classes (class struggle).[7]

Much to his surprise, however, as to that of his bourgeois ideological counterparts, "The class reductionist paradigm has proven to be more resilient; it continues to inform influential contemporary Marxist discussion of the national question."[8]

Earlier, in an effort to reformulate Marxist theory to account for certain political/ideological phenomena such as nationalism, Otto Bauer conceptualized the nation and nationalism as an idea that is an autonomous force independent of class and class struggle—a position that was strongly criticized and rejected by Lenin and other classical Marxists.

More recently, Horace B. Davis attempted to develop a similar theory that gave equal weight to class and nation as forces that are functional in separate spheres of social consciousness in a parallel fashion.[9] Despite Davis's otherwise fine historical analysis of the issues surrounding the origins and development of nationalism, his attempt to revise Marxist theory to accommodate the nationalist problematic by assigning to it an autonomous status has led him in a similarly idealist direction that has undermined the development of a class-based materialist analysis of nationalism and the national question.

This theoretical error stemming from the logic of such analysis is repeated by another respected scholar of Marxism of long standing, Eric Hobsbawm, who treats nationalism in similarly idealist terms.[10] Hobsbawm's view that nationalism is an irrational, invented ideology that is based on an imaginary allegiance to the nation independent of any direct link to class and social processes places him, like Davis, in the company of critics such as Nairn, Anderson, Laclau, and Nimni, who have criticized classical Marxism for its "class reductionism."

Notwithstanding these criticisms, the present study makes a further contribution to a class-based Marxist theory of nationalism, the national question, and national movements—one that is firmly rooted in *class* and *class struggle* as the motive force of social change and social transformation.

THE CLASS NATURE OF
NATIONALISM AND NATIONAL MOVEMENTS

Contrary to the distorted critique of classical Marxism by some self-styled "Marxists" who have turned to bourgeois, idealist modes of thought for answers, I argue here that nationalism and national movements are phenomena that cannot be studied in isolation without taking into account the social and class structure of the society in which they arise. National and ethnic divisions (as well as nationalist ideology, as an extension of such divisions) are manifestations of class conflicts and class struggles that are at base a reflection of social relations of production.[11]

"National relations," writes G. Glezerman, "cannot be understood outside of and independently of class relations." "This being the case, a class approach is one of the most important features inherent in the methodology of the Marxist analysis of social phenomena, including nations, national interests and national movements."[12]

"The division of society, or a nation, into classes," Glezerman continues, "and the division of humanity into nations, nationalities, etc., have different historic roots. Yet relations between nations and classes cannot be viewed in isolation from each other."[13]

> Nations like classes are connected with a definite set of conditions of the material life of society. The material elements characteristic of a nation are common territory and, what is most important, a community of economic life which unites all parts of the nation into a single whole. A nation is also characterized by the specific features of its spiritual life, certain national traits, a single language and national consciousness.[14]

Karl Marx and Frederick Engels devoted much time and effort to the study of the nature and dynamics of nationalism and the national question. Their analyses of the Irish national question, the anticolonial revolts in India, and national uprisings elsewhere in Asia and the Middle East, as well as in other parts of the world, show the scope and depth of their understanding of the nature and role of national movements and struggles for national self-determination that they viewed to be part of the worldwide proletarian struggle against capitalism.[15]

Subsequently, V. I. Lenin, through his perceptive political analysis in linking the national and colonial questions to the worldwide expansion of imperialism, Marxist discourse on the national question and the right of nations to self-determination, took on its political significance as an aspect of the class struggle to facilitate the fight for socialism and social emancipation.[16]

Lenin's theses on the national and the colonial questions were closely connected to his analysis of modern imperialism as the highest stage of capitalism. And this linkage, which laid bare the imperialist domination and oppression of colonized peoples and nations, led to the consequent response that set the stage for the struggle for national liberation.[17]

J. V. Stalin, following this tradition established by the Marxist classics, addressed the national question most directly by focusing on the concept of *nation* as the centerpiece of his study and analysis of nationalism and national self-determination. In "Marxism and the National Question," Stalin summed up the characteristic features of a nation this way: "A nation is a historically constituted, stable community of people, formed on the basis of a common language, territory, economic life, and psychological make-up manifested in a common culture."[18]

Placing it in historical context, Stalin situated the concept of nation within the framework of the evolution of capitalism and the capitalist state. With the expansion of capitalism on a world scale, and with the impact of capitalist imperialism on the colonies and neocolonial territories that capitalism came to dominate throughout the world, Marxist theory subsequently incorporated during the period of the Third International a broader definition of the rise of nations and national movements that corresponded to developments in the latest stage of capitalist development—the age of modern imperialism. Thus, a broader reconceptualization of the national question and national self-determination that would include nations colonized and oppressed by imperialism provided the basis of a modified Marxist theory of nationalism that became the classic statement of the Marxist position on this question during the twentieth century.

In this context, "The very processes of the formation of nations, the development of the national liberation movement, and the rise of national states," writes Glezerman, "cannot be correctly understood without taking into consideration the class or classes which determine the social content of these processes and are their motive force."[19] Thus, "Nations as well as classes come into existence on the basis of the objective process of social development."[20]

Marxist theory points out that the specific nature of class relations, which are based on relations of production, come to inform the nature and content of political struggles; such struggles, when they occur at the *inter*-national level, take the form of *national* struggles. Thus, while exploitative relations between two contending classes within a national territory take the form of an internal class struggle, a similar relationship at the international level manifests itself in the form of a national struggle. This struggle, which is the national expression of an international class struggle, is led by a particular class and is often based on an alliance of several classes unified for a common goal—national liberation and self-determination.[21]

The nature of the process for self-determination, which is characteristic of Third World anti-imperialist national liberation struggles, is quite different in the advanced capitalist imperial centers of Europe and North America. In these regions, the struggles waged by national minorities against the central state tend to be demands for limited autonomy, self-rule, or similar such status within the boundaries of the larger federal structure—demands that fall short of full national independence and statehood. This has been the case, for example, in Quebec and the Basque Country, as well as Puerto Rico and Northern Ireland.[22]

In yet other instances, when the national question is raised within the context of a socialist state, we find an entirely different dynamic at work. In some cases, such as in China, nationalities policy may be framed within the context of national integration, which at the same time recognizes cultural diversity and allows regional autonomy to various ethnic and nationality groups. In other cases, such as in the former Soviet Union, some national groups may come to play a disproportionately dominant role, where the center fails to deal with deep-seated national antagonisms inherited from an earlier period, which in time may give rise to the disintegration of the central state along national lines. However, while long-suppressed national aspirations under an otherwise seemingly cooperative federated state may engender nationalism and ethnic conflict, such as in the conflict between Armenia and Azerbaijan, it is important to stress again that here too a closer examination of these conflicts reveal the class nature of national struggles often fueled by long-standing ethnic and religious divisions.[23]

NATIONALISM, NATIONAL MOVEMENTS, AND CLASS STRUGGLE

A few key substantive questions that lie at the heart of nationalism must be briefly raised to sort out the class nature of national movements and struggles for national self-determination. Thus, while all national movements possess characteristics that are historically specific, the central question that must be raised as theoretically applicable to all such struggles for national liberation is the necessity of a *class analysis approach* to the study of nationalism.

Nationalism, writes Albert Szymanski in his book *Class Structure*, "is the ideology that members of a nation, people, ethnic group, or 'racial' minority have more in common with each other than the various constituent classes of the group have with other people in similar class positions."[24] Moreover,

"nationalism" dictates that because of their postulated overriding common interest, all classes within the ethnic group, people, or "racial" minority should work together economically and politically to advance their collective interests *against* other "nations," "races," ethnic groups, or peoples (even against those who are in the *same* classes). Nationalism is the advocacy of ethnic or "national" solidarity and action over class consciousness and action. It is, thus, the opposite of class consciousness that argues solidarity should occur and political alliances be formed primarily along *class* lines (even against the relatively privileged groups within one's subordinate ethnic group). Nationalism and class consciousness are, thus, alternative strategies of political action for gaining improvement in one's life.[25]

"In fact," adds Szymanski, "nationalism is a product of class forces. Although different kinds of nationalism differ qualitatively in their effects, *all* serve some classes within a given racial or ethnic group as opposed to others."[26]

The adoption of a class analysis approach to the study of nationalism, therefore, would entail an analysis of the class base of a particular national movement, the balance of class forces within it, and the class forces leading the movement. On this basis, one could determine the nature and future course of development of a national movement and whether a given movement is progressive or reactionary. Once the *class character* of a liberation movement and its leadership is thus determined, a political differentiation of various types of national movements can be ascertained, which in turn would provide us with clues to the social–political character of the movement in question.[27]

An understanding of the class nature of a given national movement may also inform us of the nature of the class forces that movement is struggling *against*, hence the nature and forms of the class struggle. The class content of the anti-imperialist liberation struggle, then, transforms the national struggle into a *class* struggle, which is fought at the national and international levels.

This struggle, which appears in the form of a national struggle, is, in essence, a *struggle for state power*.[28] "If national struggle . . . is class struggle, [i.e.,] . . . one very important form of the struggle for state power," writes James Blaut, then a number of questions arise that are central to an understanding of nationalism and a national movement: "Which classes make use of it, in which historical epochs, and for which purposes?"[29] Thus, through such an analysis, one can expect a relationship between the class character of a national movement, its political goals, and the nature and direction of the postindependence state following a successful national struggle.

In national struggles led by the petty bourgeoisie, for example, the class position of this segment of Third World societies often lead to an anti-imperialist liberation struggle in which the petty bourgeois forces play a dominant role. In such situations, writes Szymanski,

> Both sectors of the petty bourgeoisie tend to become nationalist because of their feelings of social humiliation and lack of fundamental control over their lives— a situation they can easily attribute to foreign domination. This class becomes disillusioned with the authoritarian rule of the transnational-local capitalist coalition. Its tendency is to increasingly support various nationalist opposition movements often in alliance with the working class and peasantry—movements to which they attempt to provide leadership.[30]

"The nationalist propensities of the petty bourgeoisie," Szymanski continues, "are felt especially strongly in the intelligentsia":

> Those whose lives center on learning, teaching, writing, and art have an especially strong identification with the idea of the nation, and an especially strong resentment of foreign cultural and economic domination. This is both because of their own material interest in advancing their careers, and because of their genuine feelings of offended dignity as the representative of an oppressed culture. Similar feelings of national humiliation are experienced by junior military officers who sense their nation's economic (and thus military) inferiority and the subordination of their countries. . . . This intelligentsia and/or junior officer strata of the petty bourgeoisie often lead anti-imperialist movements that have sometimes succeeded in defeating imperialist influence, local allies of imperialism in the bourgeoisie, and the incipient national bourgeoisie to establish essentially petty-bourgeois states.[31]

This same process under the leadership of another class, for example, leads to a completely different outcome in favor of the class that succeeds in taking state power. In either case, the important question once again becomes the class nature of the social forces that wage the struggle for national liberation and lead the rest of society in a particular political direction.

NATIONALISM, CLASS STRUGGLE, AND SOCIAL TRANSFORMATION

National movements that are struggling for self-determination are also engaged in struggles against dominant class forces that are in control of the prevailing social system. As a result, national struggles often turn into class struggles where a subordinate, oppressed class comes to express its interests through a revolutionary movement aimed at taking state power. Such a movement is often led by a single class or an alliance of class forces whose interests are opposed to those who control the state. Thus, as I have pointed out elsewhere:

> Class forces mobilized by the petty bourgeoisie and other intermediate sectors of society . . . have seized power by rallying people around a nationalist ideology directed against imperialism and its internal reactionary allies, the landlords and compradors. . . . [R]evolutions led by worker-peasant coalitions against imperialism and local reaction have resulted in the establishment of socialist states.[32]

Hence, a national movement led by the national or petty bourgeoisie, that is, bourgeois nationalism, can, when successful, set the stage for the building of a national *capitalist* state; an anti-imperialist national movement that is led by the working class in alliance with the peasantry, on the other hand, can, upon waging a successful national liberation struggle, begin building a popular *socialist* state.[33] In other instances, actions by a coalition of class forces that mobilizes a variety of social classes through cross-class alliances aimed at capturing state power may, due to the absence of a clearly articulated class position, result in the transformation of society in an "ambiguous" direction, such that in the absence of a clear and resolute action against existing social, political, and economic institutions of society, the new order may soon lose its dynamism and become incorporated into the structures of the global political economy dominated by the imperialist states.

Given the dominant role of imperialism today, it is important to recognize the force brought to bear by the imperialist states in shaping the nature and direction of such movements that have an immense impact on the balance of class forces at the global level. Such intervention by an external force becomes a crucial determinant of the class struggle when it is articulated through various internal class forces that are allied to it. An alliance of dominant classes at the global level is thus aimed at blocking the struggles of national movements in an effort to forestall the development of the class struggle that would transform the state and society and bring to power forces whose interests are contrary to and clash with those in control of the prevailing social order.

The critical factor that distinguishes the nature and dynamics of contemporary forms of nationalism and national movements, then, is the *class character* of these movements and their *class leadership*. It is within this context of social–political developments in the struggle against the existing state and social–economic structures of society that we begin to delineate the nature and dynamics of ongoing class struggles and social transformations embarked upon by movements determined to succeed in gaining national liberation and self-determination.

CONCLUSION

The diverse settings in which struggles for autonomy, self-determination, and national liberation take place necessitate a careful analysis of the relationship between class, state, and nation—phenomena that are central to our understanding of the nature and dynamics of nationalism, class struggle, and social transformation. It is thus within the framework of an understanding of the relationship between these phenomena that we find the social relevance of nationalism and national movements as manifested in different spatial, temporal, and political contexts. An analysis of the class nature of national movements, then, provides us a clear understanding of the nature, form, and class content of nationalism, as well as the nature and dynamics of the society that a given movement is struggling to build. With a clear class perspective on the ideology of nationalism and national movements, we can thus better comprehend this powerful and persistent phenomenon that has gripped the attention of the world community throughout the twentieth century.

NOTES

1. Tom Nairn, *The Break-Up of Britain*, 2nd ed. (London: Verso, 1981), p. 329.

2. Nairn, *The Break-Up of Britain*, p. 329.

3. Benedict Anderson, *Imagined Communities: Reflections on the Origin and Spread of Nationalism* (London: Verso, 1983), p. 13.

4. Ernesto Laclau, "Preface," in Ephraim Nimni, *Marxism and Nationalism: Theoretical Origins of a Political Crisis* (London: Pluto Press, 1991), p. x.

5. Nimni, *Marxism and Nationalism*, p. 4.

6. Nimni, *Marxism and Nationalism*, p. 10.

7. Nimni, *Marxism and Nationalism*, p. 10.

8. Nimni, *Marxism and Nationalism*, p. 10. See, for example, Jeff Pratt, *Class, Nation, and Identity* (Herndon, Va.: Pluto Press, 2003).

9. Horace B. Davis, *Toward a Marxist Theory of Nationalism* (New York: Monthly Review Press, 1978).

10. Eric Hobsbawm, *Nations and Nationalism since 1780* (Cambridge, U.K.: Cambridge University Press, 1992).

11. See Albert Szymanski, *Class Structure: A Critical Perspective* (New York: Praeger, 1983), pp. 5–7, 76–84.

12. G. Glezerman, *Classes and Nations* (Moscow: Progress Publishers, 1979), pp. 7–8.

13. Glezerman, *Classes and Nations*, p. 21.

14. Glezerman, *Classes and Nations*, p. 15.

15. Karl Marx and Frederick Engels, *On Colonialism* (New York: International Publishers, 1972).

16. V. I. Lenin, "Imperialism: The Highest Stage of Capitalism," in *Selected Works*, Vol. 1 (Moscow: Foreign Languages Publishing House, 1960).

17. V. I. Lenin, "Preliminary Draft Theses on the National and the Colonial Questions," in *Collected Works*, Vol. 31 (Moscow: Progress Publishers, 1966). See also: V. I. Lenin, "The Right of Nations to Self-Determination," in *Collected Works*, Vol. 20 (Moscow: Progress Publishers, 1964); V. I. Lenin, "Critical Remarks on the National Question," in *Collected Works*, Vol. 20 (Moscow: Progress Publishers, 1964); and V. I. Lenin, "The Socialist Revolution and the Right of Nations to Self-Determination: Theses," in *Collected Works*, Vol. 22 (Moscow: Progress Publishers, 1964).

18. Joseph Stalin, *Marxism and the National Question* (New York: International Publishers, 1934).

19. Glezerman, *Classes and Nations*, p. 21.

20. Glezerman, *Classes and Nations*, p. 11.

21. James M. Blaut, *The National Question: Decolonizing the Theory of Nationalism* (London: Zed Books, 1987), pp. 176–95, argues that national liberation struggles against imperialism are, in essence, class struggles that take place at the international level.

22. See Berch Berberoglu, ed., *The National Question: Nationalism, Ethnic Conflict, and Self-Determination in the Twentieth Century* (Philadelphia: Temple University Press, 1995), for a series of case studies on the national question in the advanced capitalist countries.

23. Berberoglu, *The National Question*, pp. 227–314.

24. Szymanski, *Class Structure*, p. 430.

25. Szymanski, *Class Structure* (emphases in the original).

26. Szymanski, *Class Structure* (emphasis in the original).

27. See Berch Berberoglu, *The Internationalization of Capital: Imperialism and Capitalist Development on a World Scale* (New York: Praeger, 1987), chap. 7. See also, Berch Berberoglu, *Political Sociology: A Comparative/Historical Approach*, 2nd ed. (New York: General Hall, 2001), chap. 2.

28. Berberoglu, *The Internationalization of Capital*. See also, Blaut, *The National Question*, pp. 23, 46, 123.

29. Blaut, *The National Question*, pp. 4, 46.

30. Albert J. Szymanski, *The Logic of Imperialism* (New York: Praeger, 1981), p. 426.

31. Szymanski, *The Logic of Imperialism*, p. 427.

32. Berberoglu, *Political Sociology*, p. 112.

33. Berberoglu, *Political Sociology*, p. 112.

Part Two

NATIONALISM AND ETHNIC CONFLICT IN THE AGE OF GLOBALIZATION

Chapter Three

Nationalism and Ethnic Conflict on a World Scale: Global Comparisons

During the course of the twentieth century, there have been several major forms of national domination that have historically given rise to nationalism and national movements struggling for national liberation. First is the dispossession of a people through colonial and imperial domination, occupation, and carving out of their historic homeland, reducing them to a subject population, as in the Western colonial and imperialist domination and enslavement of the African people through the slave trade. Later, the peoples of the Americas, Asia, and the Middle East came under similar forms of domination and rule, culminating in the occupation and partition of various territories through a series of mandates, as in the partition of the Ottoman Empire by the Western imperialist powers and the dispersion of its native populations, which led to the current predicament of the Palestinian and Kurdish peoples.

Second is the denial of the right to national self-determination to peoples dominated by the imperial state in the advanced capitalist countries. These include the domination of Northern Ireland by British imperialism, of Puerto Rico by U.S. imperialism, of the Basque Country by Spain, and of Quebec by the Canadian state, among others. A related situation within the advanced capitalist countries involves the oppression of immigrants and ethnic and racial minorities, such as Native Americans, African Americans, and Mexican Americans in the United States and Algerians, East Indians, Arabs, Turks, and others in France, Britain, Germany, and other advanced capitalist countries in Europe and elsewhere. Third, and more recently, in the aftermath of the collapse of socialism in Eastern Europe and the former Soviet Union during the past decade, we have seen the rise of right-wing reactionary forces in these countries that have found the opportunity to capture state power through ethnonationalist mobilization, targeting an increasingly ineffective and weakened socialist state that came under pressure during the cold war years of the postwar global capitalist political economy. Here, as in the case of the former Yugoslavia, the ensuing ethnonational conflict has led to ethnic strife and civil war.

Let us take up each of these cases briefly and highlight the dynamics of the process that affects the nature and forms of national identity and expression culminating in ethnonational conflicts that have fostered the emergence and development of social movements for national self-determination.

NATIONALISM AND ETHNIC CONFLICT IN THE THIRD WORLD

Historically, the Spanish, Portuguese, French, Dutch, British, and later U.S. imperial powers came to confront indigenous peoples and cultures around the world that more and more came under the control and influence of the dominant Western powers and were suppressed and denied their national identity, autonomy, and self-determination.

Spanish expansion to the New World was characterized by plunder of the newly acquired colonies. As the Indian population declined, and Spain accelerated its acquisition of new territory, it became necessary to secure Indian labor to work the land. The Spanish conquerors destroyed native irrigation systems, incorporated native land into Spanish estates, and forced the evacuation of Indians from their land.[1]

Elsewhere, in Brazil, an insufficient number of Indians necessitated the importation of slaves from Africa. Thus feudal Portugal set up slavery as the dominant mode of production in its Brazilian colony in order to facilitate the extraction of precious metals and other raw materials for sale on the world market. Slaves were used first in sugarcane fields and later in mining gold and diamonds.

In the Caribbean and along the Atlantic coast of North America, a similar pattern was established. Black slaves from Africa worked the sugar and cotton plantations, while the Native Americans of these areas were displaced or physically eliminated, thus transforming local social structures.[2] In these regions, the British colonialists became the dominant force.

Large areas of Asia were colonized by Western powers until the middle of the twentieth century. British and European imperialism mercilessly plundered these regions at the height of their empires. Through their presence in the region, they effected major changes in the social and economic structures of the societies they came to dominate.

Britain assumed political sovereignty in India late in the eighteenth century. As trade with Britain increased, and the demand for Indian goods grew, local capital expanded into crafts, textiles, and industrial production. This gave rise to a renewed expansion of local manufacturing industry and with it the development of a national industrial bourgeoisie that came to be seen as a competitor with British imperialism. This prompted Britain to take steps to crush Indian industry and turn India into an appendage of its colonial economy.[3]

Antagonism between the British and local industrial capital led to the national bourgeois alliance with the peasantry to throw off the British yoke through the independence movement.[4] Much as in North America, but unlike the situation in Latin America, the national bourgeois forces were able to consolidate power and capture the leadership of the movement in a victory over the British. By the late 1940s, they installed a state committed to the development of local capitalism in India following independence. Given the relatively weak position of the national bourgeoisie, the victorious nationalist forces were able to utilize the powers of the state and establish a state capitalist regime to assist in the accumulation of capital by the Indian bourgeoisie.[5]

Although not formally colonized, China too came under the influence and control of the Western imperialist powers, as traditional forms of exploitation were reinforced through the link to Europe and other centers of Western imperialism. The Western powers intervened in China and attempted to incorporate it into the world capitalist orbit at the end of the eighteenth and the beginning of the nineteenth centuries.[6] A protracted struggle against Western imperialism followed and ushered in a period of intense nationalism that paved the way for the national bourgeois forces to capture state power by the early twentieth century.

In Africa, the European colonial powers imposed slavery and spread the slave trade throughout the continent in the sixteenth century. Slaves became Africa's major export, as they were sold to masters in various parts of the world, especially in the Americas. During this period, the African economy became highly dependent on the European colonial economy tied to the slave trade.[7]

Until the middle of the twentieth century, when most African countries won their formal independence, the local economies were a direct appendage of the colonial center, which directed development in the colonies. The pattern was based on the logic of the capitalist mode of production that dominated the economies of the center states and evolved according to its needs of accumulation, resulting in uneven development between the imperial center and the colonies, and within the colonies. This classic colonial relationship prevailed in a number of African countries after the granting of formal independence, and led to the restructuring of social–economic relations on a neocolonial basis.

Elsewhere in Africa, nationalist forces have taken the initiative to lead the newly independent states along a less dependent path. Utilizing the military and state bureaucracy as supportive institutions to carry out their development programs, the petty bourgeois leaders in these countries have opted for a state capitalist path that has corresponded well with their class vision of society and social–economic development. Nasser in Egypt, Boumediène in Algeria, Kaunda in Zambia, and Nyerere in Tanzania could be cited as prime examples of petty bourgeois nationalist leaders in charge of postcolonial states developing along the state–capitalist path.

Historically, the presence of a racist apartheid regime in South Africa has been a great impediment to the development of revolutionary forces in the southern cone of Africa and has had a major impact on the scope and pace of development on the continent in a progressive direction. With the official abolition of the apartheid regime in South Africa in the 1990s, however, the last vestiges of racist colonial and neocolonial oppression was removed, so that an open political struggle could be waged by the masses to take control of their destiny and build a new society free of oppression and exploitation that they have suffered for so long.

In the Middle East, the Ottoman Empire was the major political force until the beginning of the twentieth century. After centuries of expansion and conquest, the Ottoman state began to lose ground to rival powers in Europe during the eighteenth and nineteenth centuries and became vulnerable to pressures from the West. European powers, taking advantage of the endless wars in the empire's various provinces, found their way in through direct economic controls and military occupation of large parts of Ottoman territory, which culminated in the occupation of virtually every corner of the empire during World War I.[8]

Following the collapse of the empire at the end of the war, Britain, France, Italy, and other European powers colonized its territories and remained in control of its various provinces for several decades. From the Persian Gulf to Palestine, to the Suez Canal, down to the Arabian peninsula, and across North Africa, the Ottoman territories came under the jurisdiction primarily of Britain and France, who divided up these lands to secure trade routes, raw materials, and new markets for the expanding European-controlled world economy. The Palestinian and Kurdish national questions—two classic cases of ethnonational oppression—are a product of this imperialist division and occupation of the Middle East.[9]

The partition of Palestine and Kurdistan, as well as the rest of the Middle East that came under British and French rule, effectively dispersed or divided these two peoples from their historic homelands, subjecting them to the whims of newly emergent postcolonial states that came to power in the aftermath of World War I or following the British and French Mandates: Turkey, Iraq, Syria, Lebanon, Jordan, and Israel.[10] All were created under imperialist treaties that parceled out occupied Ottoman lands among the Western powers that came to rule over the peoples of the Middle East, including the Palestinians and the Kurds.[11]

The Palestinians came under the jurisdiction of the British and the Kurds under the jurisdiction of the French and the British, in what later became Israel, Syria, Iraq, and Turkey. The Turkish territories fell to the new Turkish nationalist government, which was able to control the Anatolian portion of the Ottoman Empire and succeeded in salvaging its core into an independent republic. The masses in some Arab territories under French and British control were able to rise up and throw off imperialist rule and declare their independence.

In Turkey, Syria, Iraq, and Iran the Kurds came under newly independent states in which they became minorities. Palestine came under the control of Israel, which emerged as an independent state at the end of the British occupation of this old Ottoman territory. Subsequently, many Palestinians were either forced to disperse to neighboring Arab states and became a minority immigrant population that constituted the Palestinian diaspora, or remained in Israel as a second-class minority population under repressive rule of the Israeli state.[12] Today, it is in these independent Middle Eastern states that the Palestinians and the Kurds have been facing the most brutal oppression and are in turn fighting for their national liberation. It is from the point of view of both of these historic events (i.e., the division of their homeland by the imperialist states and the denial of their rights as minorities in the new states in which they now reside) that the Palestinians and the Kurds came to face their predicament as oppressed national groups who lack a national homeland and a national state.[13]

The parallels between the Palestinian and Kurdish national struggles over the course of the twentieth century highlight the similarities in the experience of two ethnic and national communities that have been victims of displacement and dispersion under the rule of dominant political forces for so long. These experiences led to the development of a national identity and national movement that became the expression of the communal will of the respective communities struggling to be free. The Palestinian and Kurdish national movements thus emerged in direct response to the forces that kept them down and relegated them to outright subjugation in states hostile to their struggle for national autonomy.[14]

The national movements of both the Palestinian and the Kurdish peoples thus came to represent their aspirations for nationhood and free development of their language, culture, and very being in a setting that promoted all that they stood for as a people. But the internal divisions along class and ideolog-ical lines were at once a divisive *and* a unifying expression of maturing movements that focused on the social and political forces that would lead their people to victory in the next phase of the national struggle. However, these efforts to forge unity among various sectors of the Palestinian and Kur-dish peoples to achieve victory do not resolve the complicated situation re-garding the class character of the national movement and its leadership, nor the class nature of the movement's agenda to establish its sovereignty and the type of state and society it strives to establish after achieving independence.

As in other spheres of social life, the national movement and the struggle for national liberation is not immune to class forces and class dynamics that govern social life in class-divided societies. And the Palestinian and Kurdish national movements are not exceptions to this rule. A class analysis of the ori-gins and development of the Palestinian and Kurdish national movements (provided in chapter 4) will further explore the dynamics and contradictions of this process at greater length as two prominent cases of nationalism and ethnic conflict in the Third World.

NATIONALISM AND ETHNIC CONFLICT IN THE ADVANCED CAPITALIST COUNTRIES

In the advanced capitalist countries, the national question and ethnonational conflict have continued to be central components of racial and ethnic rela-tions for centuries. Beginning with the slave trade that accompanied the loot-ing and enslavement of Africa by the Western colonial powers, entire popu-lations of diverse ethnic origin were transported across the oceans to exploit their labor in the vast plantations and mines of the colonies.[15] Africans, Na-tive Americans, and indigenous populations across the world came under this global assault of the colonizers as the latter engaged in the plunder of native lands and the exploitation and oppression of natives in distant outposts, which served to further the economic expansion of the colonial and imperial cen-ters.[16] Thus, a dual process of domination of racial and ethnic minorities be-gan to unfold as the lands and peoples of the conquered territories (as in the case of the Americas) came under colonial control, while others were brought in from distant colonial outposts to the imperial heartland to generate wealth through the use of slave labor.[17] Although the North American Indians did not make good slaves, they did nonetheless become subjugated by the white Eu-ropean colonists as the indigenous populations of North and South America came under the direct control of the British, French, Spanish, Portuguese, and other European colonial powers at different periods in history, during which new colonial empires were built on the backs of the exploited and oppressed peoples of the continent. In this process of plunder and enslavement, millions of natives perished through a combination of factors that together resulted in a genocide of unprecedented proportions, leading to an enormous decline in native populations throughout the Americas.[18]

The conquered Native American populations, north and south, were supplanted by a steady flow of African slaves brought to labor in the mines and fields across the U.S. South and the Caribbean basin, who in time became part of the local population, albeit as second-class citizens whose worth rarely exceeded that of three-fifths of their white colonial counterparts. Together, the Native American and black African American peoples came to constitute the basis of the early minority population in North America, with a varied combination of their mestizo, mulatto, as well as native sisters and brothers in the rest of the continent, who also came under severe discrimination over the course of centuries of exploitation and oppression under colonial and imperial rule—first by foreign and later by local ruling classes of European origin.[19]

Later, during the Spanish occupation of North America and following the Mexican-American war of the mid-nineteenth century, the United States inherited a Mexican population of native-born Chicanos and Mexican immigrants who came to constitute another major ethnic group in the new nation-state in formation that came to encompass the fifty states of the United States of (North) America.[20]

Hence, the Native American, African American, and Mexican (or Hispanic) American populations formed the three main minority populations of the United States. Notwithstanding the steady flow of immigrants from various European, Asian, and other countries who came to America in the nineteenth and the turn of the twentieth centuries, adding to the diversity of the U.S. population, these three major racial/ethnic groups came to define the nature of racial/ethnic relations in the United States over the course of the twentieth century.[21]

While the struggles of colonized peoples like Native Americans, Puerto Ricans, Hawaiians, and others under the U.S. yoke bring up the national question, the racist oppression visited upon colonized peoples and immigrants in the imperial heartland, wherein they have been reduced to powerless minorities treated as second-class citizens, confronts the tensions surrounding racial and ethnic relations that are part of domestic, national life within the confines of established nation-states like the United States.[22]

These dual problems of racial/ethnonational conflict that define the parameters of both the national question *and* domestic racial/ethnic relations confronting the advanced capitalist countries are not restricted to the United

States alone; they are, in fact, the creation of the major European colonial and imperial powers like Britain, France, Belgium, Italy, Spain, Portugal, the Netherlands, and others who are responsible for colonial plunder and occupation of distant native lands.[23] The problems that these powers face with their own racial/ethnic minority populations at home, who were either forcefully brought in from the colonies to supplant local labor or have (through their economic, political, cultural, and educational links with the colonies) immigrated to the colonial/imperial centers, stem from the legacy of colonialism that has created the conditions for the racial/ethnic strife that these countries now confront in their midst. Thus, East Indians, Africans, Middle Easterners, Caribbean islanders, and others in Britain; Algerians, Tunisians, Moroccans, and other African and Middle Eastern immigrants in France; and a variety of other peoples from the ex-colonies of Spain, Portugal, Italy, Germany, Belgium, the Netherlands, and other European powers who carved out Africa, Asia, the Middle East, and the Americas all represent the historic end result of colonial and imperial domination that has created this dual problem of the national question, on the one hand, and domestic racial/ethnic oppression, on the other, that have affected colonized and oppressed peoples everywhere.

While the oppression of ethnic minorities in the advanced capitalist centers continues to be the main source of racial/ethnic tensions at home, the occupation of ethnonational territory by the chief imperialist states, such as the British occupation of Northern Ireland, U.S. occupation of Puerto Rico, Israeli occupation of Palestine, and the domination of Basques in Spain and Quebecois in Canada, continues to foster struggles for national liberation as the basis of resolving the national question in the advanced capitalist countries.

NATIONALISM AND ETHNIC CONFLICT IN EASTERN EUROPE AND THE FORMER SOVIET UNION

Transformations in Eastern Europe and the former Soviet Union during the 1990s fueled the upsurge in national rivalries and led to ethnic conflict and civil war. The rise of nationalism and nationalist movements in Eastern Europe and the former Soviet Union in the aftermath of the collapse of socialism during the past decade came about when right-wing bourgeois forces in these countries succeeded in capturing state power through ethnonationalist mobilization directed against the weakened socialist states that were under constant assault by the capitalist West during the cold war years of imperialist expansion.

Under socialism, the multitude of nationalities and ethnic groups in Eastern Europe and the former Soviet Union lived in peace and progressed within the context of a cooperative social environment in which minority culture and values were protected. The customs, traditions, languages, and ways of life of these groups were promoted within the boundaries of socialism and social life that brought together these diverse nationalities under one roof, cultivating cooperation and diffusing conflict as part of the process of progress toward full communism. But, with the collapse of socialism and communist rule in Eastern Europe and the former Soviet Union during the past decade, these former socialist states have been in turmoil and embroiled in violent ethnonational conflict and civil war that has been tearing down their societies. The most violent and bloody of these conflicts have occurred in traditionally peaceful regions of Eastern Europe and the former Soviet Union (namely, Yugoslavia and the Transcaucasian republics of Armenia and Azerbaijan).[24]

Why? Why have formerly peaceful regions that lived in harmony for years suddenly erupted in flames and caused wars and destruction and despair? What social forces are responsible for this predicament and for what results? How and why have these forces succeeded and imposed their rule on society and unleashed a reign of terror over the people to maintain their dominance and to prolong their rule?

The social forces that stand to benefit from the recent developments in Eastern Europe and the former Soviet Union have been able to mobilize a considerable amount of support to deal with problems of the post-Soviet transition to a private market-oriented economy. Such mobilization has served a dual purpose: to protect the interests of a newly privileged dominant class *and* to channel the discontent of the general population in a right-wing, ultranationalist direction that can be controlled and regulated. At the same time, the economic crises that these countries have been facing in this period of transition have led to enormous material deprivation of broad segments of the population,[25] and this has been the primary factor for the emergence of ultranationalist movements. Mindful of the declining living standards of the general population, while enriching themselves through legal and illegal means (especially through government corruption), the newly emergent dominant groups have promoted right-wing reactionary activity to fan the flames of ethnic strife as a means of social control. But behind the ethnonational conflicts that are fostered by these forces, characteristic of this period, it is increasingly becoming evident that such conflicts are deeply rooted in socioeconomic relations that are at base *political* in nature—that is, struggles for political power.

Looking at the situation in Yugoslavia, one is struck by the fact that this once peaceful multiethnic and multinational society of diverse cultures and religions was forced into senseless conflict, hatred, and civil war. The forces that pushed Yugoslavia into civil war and subsequently caused its destruction were those that wanted Yugoslavia to be dismembered, broken up, and turned into a series of weak dependent states—dependent on the West.[26]

The partition of Yugoslavia and dismemberment of its constituent parts into small independent states served rival capitalist interests in the Balkans and that led to an all-out war against the last remaining territory of the former Yugoslav state (Serbia) following the secession of Slovenia, Croatia, Macedonia, and Bosnia-Herzegovina. If one were to examine the Yugoslav case and explore the social forces behind this conflict, one would inevitably draw the following conclusions:

1. The opposition forces fighting the central government were clearly anti-communist.
2. These right-wing reactionary forces used nationalism as a cover to achieve capitalist ends.
3. They were aided by external imperialist powers in order to topple the existing socialist regime and replace it by a capitalist one tied to the West.
4. By stirring up entire populations through nationalist propaganda to serve narrow capitalist ends, they were able to pit one segment of the population against another, and capture power through the practice of divide and conquer.
5. Separatist action and secession from the Federation well served the reactionary forces who wanted to establish their own separate capitalist state to exploit the masses for private gain and link their future to the Western imperialist states.
6. The partition of Yugoslavia and dismemberment of its constituent parts into small independent states advanced Western interests in the Balkans and led to an all-out war against the last remaining territory of the former Yugoslav state (Serbia) by U.S. and Western intervention in Kosovo and the bombing of Belgrade, forcing the Serbs to surrender.
7. And, finally, the imperialist armies and the internal right-wing opposition cultivated by Western intelligence (as in CIA assistance to the anti-Serbian forces, through such criminal organizations as the Kosova Liberation Army, KLA),[27] were successful in bringing down Milosevic and his regime and thus succeeded in incorporating Yugoslavia into the Western capitalist orbit, subjugating the country and its people to Western capital and its internal reactionary agents.

Through this process (a process based on intense social conflict), the fate of Yugoslavia was decided in favor of one group (the right-wing bourgeois forces) against another (the working class and the masses). The new rulers of Yugoslavia represent the interests of a rising bourgeois elite that has entered the political scene with Western assistance. With the secessionist republics of Slovenia, Croatia, Macedonia, and Bosnia-Herzegovina becoming integrated into the Western orbit, the United States has succeeded in transforming Yugoslavia to serve as a key power broker in the Balkans to advance Western imperialist interests.

The former Soviet Union likewise went through a similar process of upheaval and ethnic conflict that led to open war in various parts of its vast territories. The war in Chechnya, pitting rebel groups against the Russian army, was dwarfed by the all-out war between two former Soviet republics in the Transcaucasian region—Armenia and Azerbaijan.

The rapid changes set into motion by the collapse of the Soviet Union during the early 1990s prompted a number of former Soviet republics in the Transcaucasian region and elsewhere to assert themselves in seeking national independence, cultural freedom, and political autonomy. Such political assertion, under the leadership of a series of right-wing nationalist movements, gained these republics their formal political independence in the form of a sovereign nation-state. Deep-seated national sentiments throughout the Transcaucasian region, which go back several decades and were kept in check during Soviet times, subsequently led to the violence centered around the hostilities between Armenia and Azerbaijan in the territorial dispute over Nagorno-Karabagh, an Armenian enclave within the boundaries of the former Soviet republic of Azerbaijan.[28]

The war between Armenia and Azerbaijan over Nagorno-Karabagh led to much bloodshed and destruction. Ultranationalist forces on both sides fanned the flames of violence to achieve narrow national ends, rather than working out a solution to alleviate a situation that did not need to get out of hand and cause so much pain and suffering. Chauvinist bourgeois elements on the Azeri side and various nationalist forces on the Armenian side, with memories of the 1915 Armenian genocide perpetrated by the then Ottoman Turkish government (now allied with the Azeri state), went to war to settle their differences over a piece of territory that cost much in human lives.

The intense nature of the conflict between these two newly independent states brought to the surface long-suppressed national aspirations of ethnic identity and self-determination among Armenians and Azeris, which go to the heart of the phenomenon of nationalism.[29] Nationalist movements in this region of the world, led by right-wing reactionary forces, thus found an opening to assert themselves to give expression to popular national feelings that are deep in the collective psyche. Ethnonational conflicts, emerging from pent-up popular drives for national identity and self-determination, are thus the outcome of the clash of national interests articulated by organized political forces that are determined to advance their own narrowly defined national agenda. And the conflict between Armenia and Azerbaijan, no less than the conflict in the former Yugoslavia, confirms this particular feature of nationalism and ethnonational strife.

National chauvinism in these rival former Soviet republics tore down the decades-long peaceful coexistence that the socialist state had worked so hard to achieve since its inception in the 1920s. The forces of reactionary bourgeois nationalism and national chauvinism thus created once again the material basis for competition and conflict over territory, language, religion, and other forms of national identity that bourgeois nationalism cultivates, which leads to inevitable conflict and crisis.

As the recent experience of Eastern Europe and the former Soviet Union amply illustrates, nationalism and nationalist movements are often used to advance narrow class interests. Nationalism, the ideology of the national and petty bourgeoisies, is an ideology that is antithetical to the interests of working people everywhere. While national mobilization against imperialism through revolutionary leadership can lead the masses to victory, as in the case of Cuba, one should not underestimate the lethal force that nationalism represents, which, in the wrong hands, can cause much devastation and bloodshed, as we have seen throughout history.

The superiority of socialism over capitalism is bound to demonstrate, in the long run, the necessity for the masses to move beyond the narrow bounds of nationalism and the national project, all too often promoted by reactionary bourgeois elements, and strive toward a collective, egalitarian future that serves the interests of all the people in a society that is free of exploitation, oppression, and inequalities that have caused, and continue to cause, so much misery. Thus, striving toward equality, in no uncertain terms, acquires its true meaning only under socialism—a fact one hopes the people of Eastern Europe and the former Soviet Union, as well as oppressed peoples everywhere, will once again rediscover in the not too distant future.

NOTES

1. Stanley J. Stein and Barbara H. Stein, *The Colonial Heritage of Latin America* (New York: Oxford University Press, 1970).

2. Eric Williams, *Capitalism and Slavery* (New York: Capricorn, 1966).

3. Hamza Alavi, "India and the Colonial Mode of Production," *Economic and Political Weekly*, August 1975.

4. See Bipan Chandra, "The Indian Capitalist Class and Imperialism before 1947," *Journal of Contemporary Asia* 5, no. 3 (1975).

5. A. I. Levkovsky, *Capitalism in India* (Delhi: People's Publishing House, 1966). See also, Berch Berberoglu, ed. *Class, State, and Development in India* (New Delhi: Sage, 1992).

6. Frances V. Moulder, *Japan, China and the Modern World Economy* (Cambridge, U.K.: Cambridge University Press, 1977), pp. 98–127.

7. Basil Davidson, *The African Slave Trade* (Boston: Little, Brown, 1961).

8. Berch Berberoglu, *Turkey in Crisis: From State Capitalism to Neocolonialism* (London: Zed Books, 1982); Fatma Muge Gocek, ed., *Social Constructions of Nationalism in the Middle East* (Albany: State University of New York Press, 2002).

9. Berch Berberoglu, *Turmoil in the Middle East: Imperialism, War, and Political Instability* (Albany: State University of New York Press, 1999).

10. Berberoglu, *Turmoil in the Middle East.*

11. Berberoglu, *Turmoil in the Middle East.*

12. Samih Farsoun and Christina Zacharia, *Palestine and the Palestinians* (Boulder, Colo.: Westview, 1997).

13. Robert Olson, ed. *The Kurdish Nationalist Movement in the 1990s* (Lexington, The University Press of Kentucky, 1996).

14. Farsoun and Zacharia, *Palestine and the Palestinians.*

15. Williams, *Capitalism and Slavery.*

16. Walter Rodney, *How Europe Underdeveloped Africa* (London and Dar es Salaam: Tanzania Publishing House and Bogle L'Ouverture, 1972).

17. Williams, *Capitalism and Slavery.*

18. Ward Churchill, *A Little Matter of Genocide: Holocaust and Denial in the Americas, 1492 to the Present* (San Francisco: City Lights Books, 1997).

19. Stein and Stein, *The Colonial Heritage of Latin America.*

20. Rodolfo Acuna, *Occupied America*, 3rd ed. (New York: Harper & Row, 1988).

21. Martin N. Marger, *Race and Ethnic Relations: American and Global Perspectives*, 5th ed. (Belmont, Calif.: Wadsworth, 2000). See also Joseph F. Healey, *Race, Ethnicity, Gender, and Class* (Thousand Oaks, Calif.: Pine Forge Press, 1995) and Andrew L. Barlow, *Between Fear and Hope: Globalization and Race in the United States* (Lanham, Md.: Rowman & Littlefield, 2003).

22. Marger, *Race and Ethnic Relations* and Healy, *Race, Ethnicity, Gender, and Class.*

23. Rodney, *How Europe Underdeveloped Africa.*

24. Jasminka Udovicki, "Nationalism, Ethnic Conflict, and Self-Determination in the Former Yugoslavia," in *The National Question: Nationalism, Ethnic Conflict, and Self-Determination in the Twentieth Century*, ed. Berch Berberoglu (Philadelphia: Temple University Press, 1995); Aleksandar Pavkovic, *The Fragmentation of Yugoslavia: Nationalism and War in the Balkans* (Hampshire, U.K.: Palgrave Macmillan, 2000); Dusan Kecmanovic, *Ethnic Times: Exploring Ethnonationalism in the Former Yugoslavia* (Westport, Conn.: Praeger, 2001); Cathie Carmichael, *Ethnic Cleansing in the Balkans: Nationalism and the Destruction of Tradition* (New York: Routledge, 2002); Suzanne Goldenberg, *Pride of Small Nations: The Caucasus and Post-Soviet Disorder* (London: Zed Books, 1994).

25. Jan Adam, *The Social Costs of Transformation in Post-Socialist Countries: The Cases of Poland, the Czech Republic and Hungary* (New York: Palgrave, 2000). See

also Laszlo Andor and Martin Summers, *Market Failure: A Guide to the East European "Economic Miracle."* (London: Pluto Press, 1998).

26. Pavkovic, *The Fragmentation of Yugoslavia*; Raju G. C. Thomas, ed., *Yugoslavia Unraveled: Sovereignty, Self-Determination, Intervention* (Lanham, Md.: Lexington Books, 2003).

27. The KLA has been heavily engaged in global crime, including drug and gun trafficking, and prostitution and sex slavery.

28. Goldenberg, *Pride of Small Nations*.

29. Goldenberg, *Pride of Small Nations*.

Chapter Four

Nationalism, Ethnic Conflict, and Self-Determination in the Third World

This chapter provides an analysis of two classic examples of nationalism, ethnic conflict, and struggles for national self-determination in the Third World, providing case studies of the Palestinian and Kurdish national movements. Focusing on the evolution of these movements, this chapter presents a detailed analysis of the political history of the Palestinian and Kurdish struggles for national autonomy and independence and an overview of the origins and development of the Palestinian and Kurdish national movements and examination of the nature and dynamics of their struggle for national self-determination. Providing an analysis of the various political tendencies within these movements, this chapter explores the impact of these struggles on the broader national question over the course of the twentieth century.[1]

Palestinian and Kurdish nationalism emerged in response to the collapse of the Ottoman Empire and the subsequent partition of the empire's territories by the Western imperialist states at the end of World War I. The artificial creation of national boundaries during the British and French Mandates that were established following the war were designed to dominate and control the region to maintain colonial and neocolonial rule throughout the Middle East. Fostering ethnic divisions and strife, the imperialist forces did everything in their power to deny the native peoples of this region their right to political autonomy and national self-determination.

PALESTINE AND THE PALESTINIANS

A prosperous, coastal province of the Ottoman Empire, Palestine came under British rule following the Ottoman collapse at the end of World War I. The British Mandate, which controlled the territory stretching from Iraq to Jordan to Palestine, forced the native (Arab) population of Palestine to live under British dictates until the middle of the twentieth century.

With the arrival of a growing number of Jewish immigrants from Europe during the British Mandate, ethnic rivalry between Arabs and Jews reached new heights in Palestine. This rivalry was fueled by Zionist aims to secure a national homeland for the Jews in Palestine following the departure of the British from this territory. The British did leave, and the Zionists succeeded in establishing a Jewish state shortly after the end of World War II, but this also marked the beginning of the Arab–Israeli conflict centered on the Palestinian question—a conflict that stemmed from the dispossession of the native Arab peoples of Palestine.[2]

Under Ottoman rule, the Palestinians had largely been part of a rural, peasant population. "By far the majority of Palestinians in the nineteenth century, perhaps over 80 percent," writes Gordon Welty, "were peasants (*fellahin*). Some cultivation was based on sharecropping, with a division of the agricultural product between peasant and the landlord of the state property (*miri*). Much was based on peasant smallholding of *miri* land."[3] However, with the increasing commoditization of agriculture, cash crops began to replace subsistence production. As a result, the rural social–economic structure began to undergo a process of transformation.

Not all Palestinians were tied to the agrarian sector, however; a small segment consisting of the privileged few lived in the cities: "[T]he cities were the home of the Palestinian elite (the *effendi*)—absentee landlords, religious officials, and various Ottoman state authorities—as well as, in the late nineteenth century, the intelligentsia."[4] With the development of industry came a change in the structure of the labor force, as an increasing number of peasants sought wage-labor employment in the ever-expanding urban areas. Thus, by mid-century, the Palestinian population had become more diverse along occupational lines and increasingly urban.[5]

In the period following the establishment of the State of Israel, millions of Palestinians were driven into exile as refugees in neighboring Arab states. "Although some of the well-to-do Palestinians who enjoyed family or business connections in other parts of the Arab world had begun to leave Palestine shortly after the United Nations General Assembly called for the partition of the country in November 1947," writes Pamela Ann Smith, "the vast majority of the refugees left after fighting broke out between the Haganah—the underground Jewish army—and Palestinian irregulars, and later, after May 14, 1948, during battles between the Haganah, the Arab Legion (Transjordan), and the armies of Egypt, Syria, and Iraq."[6]

Many initially sought safety in Lebanon, Syria, or other parts of Palestine, particularly during the heavy fighting in the Galilee in the Spring of 1948 and after the massacre of 254 villagers in Deir Yasin in April of that year. Others fled to the West Bank and Transjordan after the entry of the Arab Legion, seeking refuge in territories held by the Jordanian forces. Still others, including many from Jaffa and the southern coastal districts, sought the protection of the Egyptian army and fled to the Gaza Strip, or to Egypt itself.[7]

During this period, more than a million Palestinians took refuge in Jordan, while half a million were driven to Lebanon, over three hundred thousand to Kuwait, and nearly a quarter of a million to Syria. Another half a million dispersed to the rest of the world, including several other Arab states, Europe, and the United States. Today, there are nearly five million Palestinians across the world, including over half a million in Gaza, over a million in the West Bank, and more than three-quarters of a million within Israel itself.[8]

The overwhelming majority of the refugees from Palestine, notes Smith, "were either peasants who had owned their homes and land in Palestine, or tenant farmers and sharecroppers who had tilled plots in or near their native villages."

> Unlike those who had experienced urban life, received an education, or had business contacts abroad, the peasantry was uniquely deprived because its source of livelihood, the land, was lost. While a few were able to flee with livestock, household goods, and some agricultural tools, the lack of suitable agricultural land in the neighboring countries in which they took refuge, combined with the relatively high rates of unemployment which already existed in the agricultural sector in the host countries, meant that most of the peasant refugees were unable to escape the poverty and loss of skills that confinement in the camps over the years, and even decades, entailed.[9]

"In contrast to the peasantry," Smith continues, "those Palestinians whose assets consisted of movable property or transferable skills were often able to make a new life in exile that, with time and effort, even surpassed the standard of living they had enjoyed in Palestine."

> As a result of the wartime prosperity which had resulted from the awarding of huge government contracts from the British, the beginning of oil exporting from Haifa, a significant rise in agricultural exports to Europe, and the development of corporate forms of business, many Palestinian merchants amassed considerable wealth in the form of stocks and shares, bank deposits, cash, and financial investments abroad.[10]

According to a survey conducted by the government of Palestine in 1946, the total amount of capital owned in Palestine in 1945 was about 281 million Palestinian pounds. Of this, £P 132.6 million was owned by the non-Jewish population—with £P 74.8 million invested in land; £P 13.1 million invested in agricultural buildings, tools, and livestock; and £P 44.7 million invested in industry, stocks, and commodities or invested abroad.[11] Thus, as Smith points out, "Some 44.7 million Palestinian pounds (U.S.$179 million at 1945 exchange rates) in capital, or about 16 percent of the total capital owned in the country, was held by the non-Jewish population in the form of assets that could be transferred abroad."[12]

> Balances held in sterling accounts in London were easily accessible to those forced into sudden exile, and the release of blocked accounts held in the Palestinian branches of Barclay's Bank and the Ottoman Bank following international negotiations in the early 1950s provided additional sums for rebuilding lives in the diaspora. Some £P 10 million was estimated to have been transferred to Jordan in the form of bank deposits and cash during the same period. (The magnitude of such a sum can be gauged by the fact that this figure equaled the total amount of money in circulation in the Hashemite Kingdom at the time.)
>
> These sums enabled many Palestinians to invest in new businesses, or to reestablish their companies in neighboring Arab countries.[13]

Thus, while exiled peasants and marginalized camp residents provided the foot soldiers for the Palestine Liberation Organization (PLO) in the national struggle, the diasporan bourgeoisie played a key role in funding the PLO's armed resistance. While the PLO's dispossessed mass base maintained the organization's revolutionary posture, the exiled prosperous sectors of the movement succeeded, through their financial muscle, in exerting a conservative influence on the PLO to keep it within the boundaries of established social–economic relations. These contradictory tendencies within the organization came to determine the class nature of the movement as manifested at the highest levels of organizational leadership and set the current context and future direction of the PLO as an organization that is the expression of a national movement struggling for independence.

THE ORIGINS AND DEVELOPMENT
OF THE PALESTINIAN NATIONAL MOVEMENT

The Palestinian national movement emerged in the early twentieth century following the collapse of the Ottoman state during World War I. Although unrest in Palestine directed against both the despotic Ottoman state and Zionist encroachments into the region had begun earlier in the previous century, it intensified during the British military occupation following the war. This was further fueled by the creation of the State of Israel by the Western powers in the aftermath of the victory over Nazi Germany at the conclusion of World War II.

The initial nationalist response to British occupation emerged from the discontent of the Palestinian masses against the structure of governance under colonial rule. This, coupled with the rise in Zionist armed provocations against the Palestinians during British rule, led to the strengthening of the Palestinian national movement.[14]

"As the Palestinian opposition became increasingly intense," writes Gordon Welty, "the British successfully pursued a policy of *divide et impera*."[15]

> British interests in Palestine were geopolitical—protecting the northeastern flank of the Suez Canal, which London viewed as the lifeline of the British Empire. The Ottoman general Jamal Pasha had shown the British in January 1915 that Palestine under hostile control could be the base of an attack on the canal. Those British interests were best served by a territory that was not ethnically so unified that the threat of self-determination was genuine.[16]

Thus, through the Balfour Declaration, Britain promoted the establishment of an independent Jewish state in Palestine, which would effectively divide the territory along ethnic lines, and in this way create competition and conflict between the Arab and Jewish communities for greater control over the region. British divide-and-rule policies, Welty points out, "were not limited to manipulating intercommunal tensions. They manipulated the competition among the Palestinian *effendi* as well":

> [I]t was Ottoman policy to balance the interests of the various Palestinian groups against one another. British policy intensified this competition by playing off one against the other. In particular, they pitted the Husseini family against the Nashashibi family, to the ultimate benefit of neither.[17]

The divisions promoted between Palestinian Arab elites, as well as between the elites and the masses, further intensified British control, but this also generated widespread resistance to colonial rule.

Palestinian resistance against the British Mandatory authority greatly increased in the early 1930s with the formation of the first exclusively Palestinian political party in 1932—the Istiqlal (Independence) Party. A general strike called in late 1933 led to direct confrontation and bloodshed. This was followed by the formation of a multitude of Palestinian political parties, including the Arab Party, the National Defense Party, and the National Reform Party. The unrest that ensued in the years following the political radicalization of the population led to the general strike of April 1936 and the Great Palestinian Revolt of 1936–1939.[18] As Baruch Kimmerling and Joel S. Migdal point out:

The Great Arab Revolt in Palestine, as Arabs have called it, was . . . the first sustained violent uprising of the Palestinian national movement, and the first major episode of this sort since 1834. . . . It mobilized thousands of Arabs from every stratum of society, all over the country, heralding the emergence of a national movement in ways that isolated incidents and formal delegations simply could not accomplish.[19]

However, Kimmerling and Migdal continue, "It also provoked unprecedented counter-mobilization."

Astonished by its tenacity . . . the British poured tens of thousands of troops into Palestine on the eve of World War II. And the Zionists embarked upon a militarization of their own national movement—nearly 15,000 Jews were under arms by the Revolt's end. Inaugurating an increasingly militarist Jewish political culture, it contributed in the 1940s to a decision by Ben-Gurion and other Zionist leaders to prepare for military struggle against the Arabs rather than against the British.[20]

The British response to the rising tide of Palestinian nationalism included further arrests of Palestinian leaders and increased repression of the Palestinian Arab population. Meanwhile, Welty points out, Zionist terrorism mounted:

Irgun (the self-styled National Military organization, which split from Haganah in 1935) began to bomb Palestinian civilian targets in 1938. As the Great Revolt wound down in late 1939, the Palestinians were carefully disarmed by the Mandatory authority—but the Zionists were not.[21]

This gave the impetus for the Zionists to further arm themselves and prepare to seize state power. This effort resulted in the "mass expulsions of Palestinians from their homes and the destruction of their villages to clear the land for Zionist endeavors," says Welty, and violent acts of terror forced entire villages into submission. In April 1948, just prior to the end of the British Mandate,

Irgun, under the leadership of Menachem Begin, massacred 254 Palestinian men, women, and children at the "pacified" village of Deir Yassin near Jerusalem, and then stuffed the mutilated bodies down the village wells in an exercise in ritual pollution. Subsequently, the Zionists publicized the atrocity and promised more; the Palestinians began to flee their homes en masse.[22]

Soon after this atrocity, war broke out between the Zionist and Arab forces, which further led to the displacement of more than seven hundred thousand Palestinians. The total number of displaced Palestinians, who dispersed to the neighboring Arab states, constituted 60 percent of the 1.3 million Muslims and Christians who had resided in Palestine before 1948.[23]

> The 1948 War is called al-Nakbah (the Catastrophe) by the Palestinians, an apt characterization. Their community was shattered, the people who fled the Zionist terror were consigned to refugee camps in Lebanon, Jordan, and Gaza, hundreds of Palestinian villages were obliterated—razed to the ground—and those Palestinians who were permitted to remain within Israel after 1948 were subjected to military occupation.[24]

Thus, through this process of displacement and rule by a colonial–settler state, the Palestinians were forced to surrender their national identity and were turned into a minority in their own native homeland.[25]

PALESTINIAN NATIONALISM AND THE STRUGGLE FOR NATIONAL SELF-DETERMINATION

During the 1950s and 1960s, Palestinian nationalism took expression through the actions of several nationalist organizations that operated in the diaspora. These included the Arab Nationalist Movement (ANM), founded by George Habash in the early 1950s, and El Fatah, founded by Yasser Arafat in the late 1950s. Later, in the mid-1960s, the PLO emerged as an umbrella organization that brought together various political tendencies in the diaspora and defined the nature of the national struggle during the sixties.[26]

The emergence of the PLO and the continued presence of El Fatah gave rise to the development of the National Front for the Liberation of Palestine, which engaged in military operations against Israel beginning in the mid-1960s. Armed operations by Palestinian commandos belonging to a number of other organizations were carried out against Israel throughout the 1960s.[27] Among these, the best known was El Fatah. However, in the late 1960s, another important organization, the Popular Front for the Liberation of Palestine (PFLP), was founded. The PFLP, and later its breakaway group, the Popular Democratic Front for the Liberation of Palestine (PDFLP), became a direct rival of El Fatah, competing for support among the Palestinian masses. The sharp political focus of the PFLP and the PDFLP, with their Marxist-Leninist ideological orientation, served to differentiate them from other (bourgeois–nationalist) organizations within the Palestinian resistance. Within a short time, they came to play a prominent role within the mass movement.[28]

On a broader level, the PLO, by the early 1970s, had come to represent most of the Palestinian organizations active in the national movement. This was also a period of growth of the Palestinian movement and one that witnessed increased discussion and debate among the various movement organizations on the future course of the resistance. While this strengthened the PLO and the Palestinian cause, it also posed a challenge to the Arab states, which wished to promote their own particular national interests—a development that led to open, brutal conflict between the PLO and some Arab states. It culminated in the 1970 Jordanian massacre that came to be known as Black September, when King Hussein's army unleashed a violent attack on the Palestinians to crush their growing power and influence in the country.[29]

The shifting of its base from Jordan to Lebanon following this massacre and expulsions from Jordan did not end PLO's misfortunes, however, as it became embroiled in the Lebanese Civil War in the mid-1970s. While the left wing of the movement supported the progressive forces led by Kamal Jumblatt and the Lebanese National Front, others chose to remain outside the conflict to avoid another Jordan. Nonetheless, the PLO could not divorce itself from the ongoing war in Lebanon, which for nearly a decade consumed its efforts and set back the movement by many years.

The entanglement of the PLO in the Lebanese Civil War, and its strategic position in Lebanon as a base for its political–military actions against Israel, cost the PLO another defeat when Israel invaded Lebanon in 1982.[30] The expulsion of the PLO leadership from Lebanon that followed intensified the repression of Palestinians in the Occupied Territories and resulted in the massacre of thousands of Palestinians in the Sabra and Shatila refugee camps in Lebanon, a massacre designed to wipe out the last vestiges of PLO influence in the country.

Despite all the setbacks and defeats suffered by the PLO during the 1970s and early 1980s, the national movement maintained its momentum in continuing its struggle for national self-determination. The repression of the Palestinian people and their leadership in both Lebanon and the Occupied Territories in the aftermath of the invasion of Lebanon did not deter them from fighting for their legitimate rights.[31] In fact, such repression increased their resolve to rise up against the forces of oppression in mass protest. In the great Palestinian uprising of 1987 (the Intifada), tens of thousands of Palestinians rose up in Gaza and the West Bank against Israel's repressive rule in the Occupied Territories.[32] This popular, mass uprising within the boundaries of post-1967 Israel strengthened the case of the Palestinian movement in demanding a permanent solution to the occupation through local self-rule.

Such an agreement was in fact reached by the mid-1990s, when the governance of the Occupied Territories was transferred to the Palestinian Authority. But the limited nature of Israeli concessions in recognizing local autonomy in Gaza and the West Bank, as well as the continued buildup of new Israeli settlements there, complicated the situation.

With the accession to power of Ariel Sharon in Israel in 2001 and the unleashing of a reign of terror against the Palestinians to enforce an ultra-right military assault across the Occupied Territories, the fragile situation in Palestine burst once again into open warfare with direct military occupation, destruction, and massacres on the part of the Israeli state and a mass uprising, suicide bombings, and another round of struggle for liberation on the part of the Palestinians that marked the beginning of the second Intifada in the West Bank and Gaza.[33] With the escalation of violence by the Israeli military/police force against the Palestinian Authority, including the siege of Arafat's headquarters in the West Bank, the confrontation between Israel and the Palestinian people reached a new and unprecedented level of violence when entire villages and neighborhoods came under Israeli attack and occupation imposing an iron-clad military rule. This new round of atrocities carried out by Israel against the Palestinian people in 2001–2003 opened a new and bloody chapter in Israeli–Palestinian relations, fueled the unstable political situation in the region, and contributed to the continuing turmoil in the Middle East.[34] U.S. support of Israel in its all-out war against the Palestinians and the U.S. war against Iraq to recolonize the region through open military occupation have further exacerbated the crisis in the Middle East and made the situation worse with immense political, economic, and social consequences that will continue to enrage the region for years to come.

Palestinian nationalism and the Palestinian national movement have come a long way over the past several decades. Despite the deportations, massacres, and destruction they have suffered over the course of their struggle for a national homeland, the Palestinians have been determined to fight for their rights to achieve national self-determination for however long it takes to accomplish this goal.

KURDISTAN AND THE KURDS

For centuries, prior to the onslaught of the Ottoman Empire, the Kurdish people had settled in what became a vital corner of the Middle East, stretching from the mountains and hills of eastern Anatolia to the northern edge of the Mesopotamian valley. The Ottoman invasion of this territory in the sixteenth century brought with it a social transformation over the course of the following four centuries that profoundly altered the structure of social relations in Kurdish society.[35]

After the Ottomans conquered Kurdistan in the sixteenth century, they set up a vassal system throughout the Kurdish territories. This system remained in force later, albeit modified by changing historical circumstances. The tribal *aghas* (landlords) competed with each other for power and influence; a conflict by one with the central state was seen by his rivals as an opportunity for weakening him. These traditional rivalries determined later political alignments in both Iraqi and Turkish Kurdistan. . . .

Thus, historical conditions favoring ethnic cohesion among the Kurdish people were present only in rudimentary form in Kurdistan before the creation of the modern Middle Eastern states.[36]

Following the collapse of the Ottoman Empire, the territory inhabited by the Kurds came under the jurisdiction of first the Western powers and later the states that were created following European occupation. Kurdistan in this way came under the eventual control of the newly emerging nation-states of Turkey, Iraq, and Syria, as well as Iran.

The situation after the Ottoman capitulation was anything but favorable for the Kurds, as the main portion of Kurdistan remained under Turkish control. Kurdistan in Iran had already been under the rule of the Persians since 1639, and South Kurdistan, which was identical with the former Ottoman province of Mosul, came under British rule. Turkish Kurdistan and South Kurdistan became the scene of the failed attempts of the Kurds to achieve independence.[37]

Covering a land mass of some 410,000 square kilometers, the territory of Kurdistan is populated by some twenty-three to twenty-six million Kurds who call it their homeland. With about half the total Kurdish population and nearly half the total territory of Kurdistan inside its boundaries (i.e., 194,000 square kilometers), Turkey has the largest concentration of Kurds in the Middle East, about thirteen million, close to a quarter of the entire population of Turkey. The portion of Kurdistan in Iran accounts for some 125,000 square kilometers where between six and seven million Kurds (or more than 16 percent of the total population of Iran) live. In Iraq, over four million Kurds (or 28 percent of the entire population of Iraq) live on 72,000 square kilometers of land. And in Syria, some 18,000 square kilometers are populated by about one million Kurds (i.e., 9 percent of the total population of Syria). In addition, more than one million Kurds live in a number of neighboring states, including the former Soviet Union and several Arab countries, while more than half a million Kurds live abroad (mainly in Europe, especially Germany) where they have settled as migrant laborers.[38]

Traditionally, the tribe has played a central role in Kurdish society and social structure:

The Kurdish tribe is a socio-political and generally also territorial (and therefore economic) unit based on descent and kinship, real or putative, with a characteristic internal structure. It is naturally divided into a number of sub-tribes, each in turn again divided into smaller units: clans, lineages, etc.[39]

However, as Bruinessen points out, "Not all Kurds are tribal; in fact in some areas non-tribal Kurds form an overwhelming majority of the population."[40] Nevertheless, "Tribal segmentation," notes Gerard Chaliand, "dominates the whole of [Kurdish] society, since even those who are not tribalized are subject to its rules."[41] In fact, "In nearly all cases," Bruinessen agrees, "they are (or were until quite recently) subjected politically and/or economically to tribally organized Kurds, so that tribal structure is, as it were, superimposed upon quasi-feudal dominance relations."[42]

"The picture of the wild, warlike, free Kurds promulgated by European and American travelers, traders, and missionaries," writes Ferhad Ibrahim, "never corresponded with reality but rather was a part of the phenomenon of 'Orientalism'."[43] "Contrary to popular belief," Chaliand points out, "only a small fraction of the Kurdish population is nomadic."

> Most are farmers and, to a much lesser extent, stockbreeders. The mountains afford no more than a subsistence level economy, whereas the plains of Syria and Iraq provide good yields of grain. . . . As a general rule, in the mountain areas where traditional methods of farming are still used, the peasants own their land, whereas in the plains large landowners depend on tenant farmers and, increasingly, on agricultural workers.[44]

Kurdish society has undergone major social transformations during the past several decades. Its character has been changing from one tied to an isolated, semifeudal agricultural system to one connected to a capitalist, urban–industrial structure based on wage labor:

> During the last twenty years, Kurdish society has undergone profound changes which have considerably altered its traditional structures. Feudalism has broken down, nomadism has disappeared and even semi-nomadism is now practiced by only a few thousand people. As agriculture is gradually mechanized the countryside is becoming depopulated; hundreds of thousands of peasants have poured into the Kurdish towns and the big Turkish industrial cities. . . . Contact with the world of the proletarians and with progressive intellectuals is politicizing them very rapidly.[45]

The great majority of Kurds are Sunni Muslims who follow the Shafi'i school, as opposed to the Hanafite school followed by the Turks and the Arabs. However, there are Kurds who follow the teachings of the Shiite sect (especially those who live in Iran, and some in Iraq), while others are followers of the Alevi and Yezidi religions.

The Kurds have a distinct language of their own, in both spoken and written form, but its use has been banned in many of the countries they live in. The most notorious among these has been Turkey, where the use of Kurdish to communicate in any form has been illegal and severely punished until recently. The ban on the use of the Kurdish language had stemmed from the policy to limit or block communication among the Kurds, as well as to erode their cultural identity to better assimilate them into the dominant culture and society.[46]

Variations in dialect and in written language practiced by the Kurds in Iran, Turkey, and the Arab states have been obstacles to communication across national boundaries:

> There is a large number of different dialects which may be classified into a number of more or less distinct groups that are not, or only very partially, mutually understandable.
>
>   1. The northern and northwestern dialects, usually called Kurmanji (a potential source of confusion is the fact that some southern tribes also call themselves Kurmanj and consequently their language, Kurmanji, although it belongs to the southern group).
>   2. The southern dialects, often called Sorani, although Sorani properly speaking is only one of the dialects belonging to this group, which also includes Mukri, Sulaymani, and many other dialects.
>   3. The southeastern dialects, such as Sine'i (Sanandaji), Kermanshahi, and Leki. These dialects are closer to modern Persian than those of the other two groups.
>
> These dialect groups show not only considerable lexical and phonological differences but also differ significantly in certain grammatical features. . . . Besides these three groups of proper Kurdish dialects, we find two other groups of dialects spoken in Kurdistan that belong to another branch of the Iranian family . . . Zaza and Gurani. . . . It should be noted, however, that no strict boundaries exist. Dialects merge gradually; groups speaking one dialect may live among a majority of speakers of another.[47]

In addition to variations in dialect by region, there are differences in written language, as exemplified in the use of a variety of alphabets:

> The Persian-Arabic alphabet was used by all literate Kurds until the end of the First World War. Then, in the 1920s, the Bedirkhan brothers introduced the Latin alphabet, which became standard in Turkish and Syrian Kurdistan. In Iranian and Iraqi Kurdistan the Arabic alphabet was adapted to the peculiarities of the Kurdish language. In the former Soviet Union the Kurdish language was written in Cyrillic letters. The variety of alphabets and the lack of uniform Kurdish language has made intellectual communication among Kurds difficult.[48]

Despite these differences and the various cultural restrictions imposed upon them by governments under which they live, the Kurds have resisted the oppression they have suffered at the hands of repressive authoritarian regimes that rule over the Kurdish territory and have found ways in which a common bond can be developed among all Kurds in their struggle for national autonomy.

THE ORIGINS AND DEVELOPMENT
OF THE KURDISH NATIONAL MOVEMENT

The Kurdish national question, and the origins of the Kurdish national movement, goes back to the collapse of the Ottoman Empire at the conclusion of World War I, which led to the partition of Kurdistan by the Western imperialist states. Subsequently, the territories inhabited by the Kurds were divided among several newly established nations that effectively dispersed the Kurdish population across parts of the Middle East. Although the first step in the formation of the Kurdish national movement was the publication of the journal *Kurdistan* in 1898, the national struggle waged by the Kurds did not fully materialize until after the partition of Kurdistan at the end of World War I.

In Iraq, the first Kurdish revolt against the British occupation of Kurdistan took place in 1919–1920. The movement, led by Sheikh Mahmoud, aimed to create an autonomous Kurdish state, but failed to achieve it:

> In 1918 in South Kurdistan, the head of the Order of Quadiriya Dynasty in Kurdistan, Sheikh Mahmud Barzanji, declared himself *hukmdar* (ruler) of Kurdistan. Initially the British administration in Mesopotamia tolerated the attempt of the Kurdish leaders to gain independence; it had not yet decided what was to become of Mesopotamia and South Kurdistan. But in 1919 the British deprived the *hukmdar* of his power, fearing that Sheikh Mahmud would present them with a fait accompli before they were able to decide the fate of the occupied region.[49]

Although the Treaty of Sevres provided a provision (Articles 62–64) for the creation of an independent Kurdish state on Kurdish territory, this never materialized.[50] The maneuverings of the Western powers, especially Britain and France, resulted in further transfers of Kurdish land to foreign hands and prepared the grounds for a second revolt led by Sheikh Mahmoud in 1923. This uprising, however, was crushed by the British army, and the sheikh was exiled to India.

With the signing of the Treaty of Lausanne in June 1923, which superseded the Treaty of Sevres, a great portion of Kurdish territory was annexed by the new Turkish state, bringing a considerable segment of the Kurdish population under its control. In early 1924, a Turkish decree banned all Kurdish schools, organizations, and publications, including religious fraternities and schools, greatly limiting the freedom of thought and association.[51] In response, "a broad-based resistance movement formed after it became apparent to the Kurds that the new Kemalist state was a Turkish state that would not permit ethnic pluralism."[52] This prompted another widespread uprising throughout Turkish Kurdistan beginning in early 1925. As in earlier cases, the uprising was brutally crushed.

In the latter half of the 1920s and throughout the 1930s, a series of new uprisings throughout Kurdistan laid the groundwork for the subsequent upsurge in nationalist activity and resistance:

> From 1925 to 1939, the barbarities of the Turkish military forces in Kurdistan provoked constant revolts and peasant uprisings. In 1925 there was the major revolt led by Sheikh Said, then the revolts in Raman and Reschkoltan, halfway between Diyarbekir and Siirt. From 1926 to 1927 it was the turn of the populations of Hinis, Vorto, Solhan, Bingol, and Gendj to rise up against the Turks. 1928 saw uprisings in Sassoun, Kozlouk and Perwari. From 1928 to 1932 an organized insurrection broke out in the Ararat area. Finally, from 1936 to 1939 it was the inhabitants of the mountains of Dersim who were battling against the Turkish troops. Apart from the Ararat revolt and the one led by Sheikh Said, these were all local and spontaneous rebellions.[53]

In the early 1930s, the uprisings in Turkey spread to the east across the border to Iran. In 1931, a new revolt broke out in Iranian Kurdistan under the leadership of Jafar Sultan, and a similar uprising in Iraq that year—first led by Sheikh Mahmoud (who had returned from exile in India) and later under the leadership of Sheikh Ahmed Barzani—set the stage for the mass confrontation with the British, who sent in the Royal Air Force to attack the Kurdish villages and put an end to the rebellion. Subsequent uprisings in Iraq in 1933 and in Turkey in 1936–1938 were crushed, but increased nationalist activity in Iraq in the early 1940s led to further revolts in the period 1943–1945.[54]

The defeat of these revolts and the retreat of the Kurdish leadership to Iranian Kurdistan led to the founding of the Kurdish Democratic Party (KDP) in Iran in 1945. A similar organization set up by the Kurds in Iraq (the Kurdish Democratic Party of Iraq) came to play a parallel role in coordinating efforts against the repressive state in Iraq.

Heightened nationalist activity and a series of uprisings in the region during this period opened the way to the proclamation of the first Kurdish Republic of Mahabad in Iran in early 1946. However, the new republic, led by Qazi Mohammed, was destroyed only one year after its inception.[55]

The defeat of the Mahabad Republic marked the beginning of the decline of the Kurdish national movement during the next two decades. It was not until the mid-1960s that the renewed struggle of the Kurdish national movement began to pose a serious challenge to the repressive regimes ruling over Kurdish territories.

KURDISH NATIONALISM AND
THE STRUGGLE FOR SELF-DETERMINATION

Beginning in the mid-1960s and throughout the 1970s, the Kurdish national movement experienced resurgence. More and more, various leftist political organizations came to embrace the Kurdish cause as part of their overall political strategy.

In Turkey, the organizations that incorporated the Kurdish question into their program included the Workers Party of Turkey (Türkiye Işçi Partisi, TIP) and the Communist Party of Turkey (Türkiye Komünist Partisi, TKP).[56] Together with various Kurdish parties and groups active in Turkish Kurdistan, these and other leftist organizations played an important role in highlighting the Kurdish question during this period.

"In the 1970s," writes Martin van Bruinessen, "the Kurdish organizations competed in putting forward ever more radical demands. . . . Not only in the east, but all over Turkey, radical politics grew extremely violent."[57] Of all the active leftist political organizations in Turkish Kurdistan, the Workers Party of Kurdistan (Partiya Karkeren Kurdistan, PKK) was the most effective.

The PKK was founded by Abdullah Öcalan in 1978 and was active among workers and peasants throughout the Kurdish regions of eastern Turkey in the years leading to the military coup in 1980.

> The PKK's militant ideology and activities in the first two years after it was founded resulted in its rigorous persecution under the military regime. Most members of the PKK's Central Committee were not able to escape from Turkey after the coup in 1980. The arrest of part of the leadership was a heavy blow to the party. It was not until the mid-1980s that the PKK was again able to become active throughout Turkish Kurdistan.[58]

The military coup in 1980 was a great setback to the Kurdish struggle in Turkey, as the Turkish army launched a massive operation in the eastern provinces to break the back of the PKK and to neutralize the resistance movement across Turkish Kurdistan.[59] The military regime went all-out to crush the Kurdish national movement in all major Kurdish towns and villages,

imposing martial law and strict military/police control on them. As David
McDowall points out:

> In order to contain this new serious challenge, the authorities resorted to a number
> of draconian measures to curb PKK insurgency. They embarked upon mass arrests
> following any guerrilla incident. The people of south-eastern Anatolia had been
> fearful of Turkey's armed forces ever since the establishment of the Republic, but
> a new phase of terror now began. Mass arrests took place, and beatings and torture
> became a commonplace experience among the Kurdish population.[60]

The situation created by this mass repression of the Kurdish population led to
a paralysis of the Kurdish national movement in the early 1980s, but it did not
last for long.

Countering the terror unleashed by the Turkish state, the PKK launched a
guerrilla war to carry out a protracted armed struggle against the Turkish
army. This action won the party the strong support of the Kurdish masses
throughout Turkish Kurdistan.[61] By the mid-1980s, the PKK took center stage
in the national struggle by founding the Armed Forces for the Liberation of
Kurdistan and the National Liberation Front of Kurdistan, and called on all
Kurdish organizations to join forces in support of this struggle.[62]

In the late 1980s, there was a significant expansion of guerrilla operations
across Turkish Kurdistan, which contributed to the growing sympathy and support for the PKK in Kurdish villages and towns. Mass demonstrations in support of the PKK took place in several towns—especially in Cizre and
Nusaybin—in the Spring of 1990, and in towns across eastern Anatolia in
March 1991, which revealed the broad-based nature of PKK's political support.

> As in 1990 there were a number of clashes between civilian demonstrators and
> the security forces in Sirnak, Idil, Cizre, Midyat and elsewhere in early March
> 1991, and more demonstrations at *Now Ruz* (New Year) on 21 March, not only
> in Kurdistan but also in Adana, Izmir and Istanbul. In July 1991 . . . [there were]
> an estimated 20,000 protesters on the streets of Diyarbekir.[63]

The PKK's role in these and other mass actions against the Turkish army's
visible presence in the Kurdish towns has been central. Its mobilization of a
large segment of the Kurdish population to fight state repression has gained the
party recognition and respect throughout Turkish Kurdistan. In fact, as Martin
Van Bruinessen points out, "The PKK is the only Kurdish organization that has
successfully challenged the Turkish army's domination of Kurdistan."[64]

"In the circumstances prevailing today," writes Ferhad Ibrahim, "the PKK
considers violence to be the only form of resistance possible against the repressive actions of the Turkish state and the violence perpetrated by its local
Kurdish agents, the aghas and the sheikhs."[65] The PKK's armed actions

against the Turkish state, which has used a large contingent of its army to put down the resistance in Kurdistan, have generated greater participation of Kurds in the PKK. But the capture by the Turkish authorities of PKK leader Abdullah Öcalan in 1999, who has subsequently renounced independence, and the fact that the PKK is no longer engaged in armed struggle against the Turkish state have complicated the situation and thrown the Kurdish national movement in Turkey into great disarray.

In Iraq, the Kurdish national movement enjoyed a brief period of rejuvenation following the fall of the monarchy in 1958. This was largely due to the widespread backing and support the movement received from radical leftist parties, including the Iraqi Communist Party, as a way of forcing concessions from the new government. However, the Kurdish forces soon fell victim to the right-wing nationalist policies of the various Ba'th governments that came to power during the 1960s, especially after the fascist coup in 1963. The situation did not get any better after Saddam Hussein's accession to power in 1968, and the movement experienced a steady decline during the 1970s and 1980s.

For a brief period in the mid-1970s, both the Patriotic Union of Kurdistan (PUK) and the Democratic Party of Kurdistan (DPK) conducted guerrilla operations against the Iraqi state, but by the late 1970s differences over ideology and strategic questions led to a major clash that brought the alliance to an end. It opened the way to all-out government retaliation in which Kurdish villages were destroyed or depopulated in an attempt to isolate the guerrillas from their mass base in the rural areas.

"Beginning in the late 1970s," writes Ibrahim, "four events led to fundamental changes in the Kurdish national movement across Kurdistan: the collapse of the movement in Iraq; the Iranian Revolution of 1979; the military coup in Turkey in 1980; and the Iran–Iraq war, which raged on for nearly a decade."[66]

During the 1980s, the Kurdish national movement faced formidable central governments in Turkey, Iraq, and Iran. The September 1980 coup in Turkey placed Kurdish regions in eastern Anatolia under martial law, and the 1979 revolution in Iran and the Iran–Iraq War that started in 1980 forced the movement into retreat during the 1980s.

In the months following the Iranian Revolution, "there were violent clashes between Kurdish nationalists and supporters of the Islamic regime."

> The army and Revolutionary Guards occupied the cities and towns, killing hundreds in the first battles, while many others were executed after summary revolutionary "justice." Thousands of armed Kurds took to the mountains and successfully engaged the army and Guards in guerrilla warfare.[67]

The predicament of the Kurdish people in Iran was thus no better than what their counterparts had experienced in Turkey and Iraq. And the ensuing

Iran–Iraq War pitted the Kurds of one country against those of another. Thus, when Iran unleashed its violent attacks on its Kurdish minority in Iranian Kurdistan, the KDP-Iran sided with Iraq for financial and logistical support; conversely, when the Iraqi Kurds were being oppressed by the regime of Saddam Hussein, Iran gave increasing support to the DPK-Iraq in its effort to topple the Iraqi regime.[68]

As the Iran–Iraq War was winding down, the event that drew international attention to the oppression of the Iraqi Kurds was the Halabja massacre. The Iraqi government's chemical bombardment of the town of Halabja resulted in the deaths of thousands of Kurdish civilians. "Less than half a year later," writes Bruinessen,

> Iraq once again used chemical arms against its Kurdish citizens, and it has effectively used the threat of such weapons of terror ever since. Not long after a ceasefire with Iran was signed, the third and most brutal *al Anfal* offensive took place (in August 1988). It was directed against the districts controlled by the Kurdish Democratic Party, in the northernmost part of Iraq. Poison gas was used in the attack, killing thousands and causing the survivors to flee in panic.[69]

By the war's end, the Kurdish national movement was in disarray in all three countries. Paralyzed and in the worst shape ever in its decades-long struggle for independence, the movement was to face yet another setback with the onset of the Gulf War of 1991. Following Iraq's invasion of Kuwait and its subsequent defeat after massive U.S. intervention, the Iraqi Kurds were encouraged to rise up against the regime of Saddam Hussein. These opposition forces ranged from Kurdish nationalists to Shiite fundamentalists to bourgeois liberals. However, as Bruinessen points out, the planned uprising completely backfired and led to the biggest disaster yet in Kurdish history:

> [I]n March 1991, the Iraqi Kurds rose up in the most massive rebellion ever. . . . For a few weeks, a feeling of freedom prevailed; the Kurds dismantled the existing government apparatus in the north, Iraqi soldiers surrendered to the Kurds or simply went home. But then it suddenly became painfully clear that Saddam's military power had not been destroyed in the war, as had been hoped. Iraqi tanks and helicopter gunships attacked the rebellious towns. Bombardments with phosphorous and sulphuric acid, and the fear of Iraq's formidable chemical arsenal, quickly demoralized many of the Kurds, sending hundreds of thousands in panic into the mountains and towards the Turkish or Iranian borders. More than two million people—half or more of the Iraqi Kurds—fled from their homes.[70]

The cross-border mass exodus of Kurdish refugees from Iraq to Turkey and Iran effectively internationalized the Kurdish question once again, forcing the three governments to address the impact of this crisis on their internal policies regarding the Kurdish minorities.

In the decade following the Gulf War, the Kurdish parties and mass organizations have regrouped and reevaluated their role in the national struggle.[71] While variations in ideological positions continue to set apart the numerous Kurdish groups across Kurdistan, one common goal has always emerged as the binding principle that defines Kurdish identity: the collective national struggle for a free and independent Kurdistan.

The U.S. invasion and war against Iraq in March 2003 that toppled the regime of Saddam Hussein to reexert U.S. dominance over the entire Middle East for control of the region's oil, may reopen the Kurdish question to settle old disputes between the Kurds and the central state. But the outcome of such action (which has subsumed Kurdish struggles under U.S. imperial interests) may once again lead to an opposite effect that would set back efforts for Kurdish independence for years to come. In the end, it will be the Kurdish people of Iraq and of the entire region who will determine their own destiny and chart their own course of development to fulfill their national aspirations.

CONCLUSION

The displacement of the Palestinian and Kurdish peoples by the Western imperialist powers through the partition of the territories in which they lived in the aftermath of the collapse of the Ottoman Empire has been at the root of the Palestinian and Kurdish national questions. The oppression of Palestinians and Kurds in their native territories, where they have been reduced to ethnic minorities, is a direct outcome of an imperial policy that resulted in war, rebellion, and political turmoil throughout the Middle East during much of the twentieth century.

The partition of Palestine and Kurdistan, as well as the rest of the Middle East that fell under British and French rule, effectively dispersed or divided these two peoples from their historic homelands, subjecting them to the whims of newly emergent postcolonial states that came to power in the aftermath of World War I or following the British and French Mandates: Turkey, Iraq, Syria, Lebanon, Jordan, and Israel. All were created under imperialist treaties that parceled out occupied Ottoman lands among the Western powers that came to rule over the peoples of the Middle East, including the Palestinians and the Kurds. And it is now in these independent Middle Eastern states that the Palestinians and the Kurds have been facing the most brutal oppression and are fighting for their national independence.

The parallels between the Palestinian and Kurdish national struggles over the course of the twentieth century highlight the similarities in the experiences of the two ethnonational communities that have long been victims of displacement and dispersion under the rule of dominant political forces. These experiences led to the development of a national identity and national movement that became the expression of the communal will of the respective communities. The Palestinian and Kurdish national movements thus emerged in direct response to the forces that kept them down and relegated them to second-class citizenship in states hostile to their struggle for national autonomy. The national movements of both the Palestinian and Kurdish peoples came to represent their aspirations for nationhood and free development of their language, culture, and very being in a setting that promoted all that they stood for as a people. But the internal divisions along class and ideological lines were at once a divisive and a unifying expression of a maturing movement that focused on the social and political forces that would lead their people to victory in the next phase of the national struggle.

The continuing struggles of the Palestinian and Kurdish peoples in the face of much adversity is a testimony to the national aspirations of these and other oppressed peoples throughout the Middle East who are determined to fight for their right to nationhood and national self-determination until their final victory.

NOTES

1. This chapter is a slightly revised and updated version of chapter 5 of my book *Turmoil in the Middle East: Imperialism, War, and Political Instability* (Albany: State University of New York Press, 1999). Reprinted by permission.

2. Edward W. Said, *The Politics of Dispossession: The Struggle for Palestinian Self-Determination, 1969–1994* (New York: Pantheon, 1994); Samih Farsoun and Christina Zacharia, *Palestine and the Palestinians* (Boulder, Colo.: Westview, 1997).

3. Gordon Welty, "Palestinian Nationalism and the Struggle for National Self-Determination," in *The National Question: Nationalism, Ethnic Conflict and Self-Determination in the Twentieth Century*, ed. Berch Berberoglu (Philadelphia: Temple University Press, 1995), p. 16.

4. Welty, "Palestinian Nationalism," p. 17.

5. Baruch Kimmerling and Joel S. Migdal, *Palestinians: The Making of a People* (New York: Free Press, 1993), pp. 130–31.

6. Pamela Ann Smith, "Palestine and the Palestinians," in *Power and Stability in the Middle East*, ed. Berch Berberoglu (London: Zed Books, 1989), p. 157.

7. Smith, "Palestine and the Palestinians," pp. 157, 159. See also Benny Morris, *Righteous Victims: A History of the Zionist–Arab Conflict, 1881–2001* (New York: Knopf, 2001).

8. Estimates of the total number of Palestinians in the diaspora vary, but there is a general consensus among authors that it is somewhere around 4.5 to 5 million.

9. Smith, "Palestine and the Palestinians," p. 159.

10. Smith, "Palestine and the Palestinians," p. 160.

11. Government of Palestine, *A Survey of Palestine*, 2 vols. (Jerusalem: Government of Palestine, 1946), vol. 2, p. 569, cited in Smith, "Palestine and the Palestinians," p. 171.

12. Smith, "Palestine and the Palestinians," p. 160.

13. Smith, "Palestine and the Palestinians," p. 160. See also J. C. Hurewitz, *The Struggle for Palestine* (New York: Greenwood, 1968).

14. David McDowall, *The Palestinians: The Road to Nationhood* (London: Minority Rights Group, 1995). See also Francis A. Boyle, *Palestine, Palestinians, and International Law* (Atlanta: Clarity Press, 2003).

15. Welty, "Palestinian Nationalism," p. 18.

16. Welty, "Palestinian Nationalism," p. 18.

17. Welty, "Palestinian Nationalism," p. 19. See also Salim Tamari, "Factionalism and Class Formation in Recent Palestinian History," in *Studies in the Economic and Social History of Palestine in the Nineteenth and Twentieth Centuries*, ed. Roger Owen (London: Macmillan, 1982), chap. 3.

18. See Kimmerling and Migdal, *Palestinians: The Making of a People*, pp. 96–123. See also Ilan Pappe, *A History of Modern Palestine: One Land, Two Peoples* (Cambridge, U.K.: Cambridge University Press, 2004).

19. Kimmerling and Migdal, *Palestinians: The Making of a People*, p. 96.

20. Kimmerling and Migdal, *Palestinians: The Making of a People*, pp. 96–97.

21. Welty, "Palestinian Nationalism," p. 21.

22. Welty, "Palestinian Nationalism," p. 22.

23. Welty, "Palestinian Nationalism." See also Nur Masalha, *Expulsion of the Palestinians* (Washington, D.C.: Institute for Palestine Studies, 1992).

24. Welty, "Palestinian Nationalism," p. 22.

25. Said, *The Politics of Dispossession*.

26. Helena Cobban, *The Palestinian Liberation Organization* (Cambridge, U.K.: Cambridge University Press, 1984). See also Alain Gresh, *The PLO: The Struggle Within* (London: Zed Books, 1985).

27. Rosemary Sayigh, *Palestinians: From Peasants to Revolutionaries* (London: Zed Books, 1979), pp. 152–54.

28. Gerard Chaliand, *The Palestinian Resistance* (Baltimore, Md.: Penguin, 1972), pp. 84–129.

29. See John Cooley, *Green March, Black September* (London: Frank Cass, 1973), pp. 109–122.

30. James Reilly, "Israel in Lebanon, 1975–82," *MERIP Reports* 12, nos. 6–7 (September–October, 1982).

31. See Samih Farsoun, "Israel's Goal of Destroying the PLO Is Not Achievable," *Journal of Palestine Studies* 11, no. 4 (1982).

32. Zachary Lockman and Joel Beinin, *Intifada: The Palestinian Uprising against Israeli Occupation* (Boston: South End Press, 1989). See also Hayim Gordon, Rivca

Gordon, and Taher Shriteh, *Beyond Intifada: Narratives of Freedom Fighters in the Gaza Strip* (Westport, Conn.: Praeger, 2003).

33. Roane Carey, ed., *The New Intifada: Resisting Israel's Apartheid* (London: Verso, 2001). See also Wendy Pearlman, *Occupied Voices: Stories of Everyday Life from the Second Intifada* (New York: Thunder's Mouth Press/Nation Books, 2003).

34. Baruch Kimmerling and Joel S. Migdal, *The Palestinian People: A History* (Cambridge, Mass.: Harvard University Press, 2003).

35. Martin Van Bruinessen, *Agha, Shaikh and State: The Social and Political Structures of Kurdistan* (London: Zed Books, 1992), pp. 133–95. See also Abdul Rahman Ghassemlou, *Kurdistan and the Kurds* (London: Collets Holdings, 1965) and Hakan Özoğlu, *Kurdish Notables and the Ottoman State: Evolving Identities, Competing Loyalties, and Shifting Boundaries* (Albany: State University of New York Press, 2004).

36. Ferhad Ibrahim, "The Kurdish National Movement and the Struggle for National Autonomy," in *The National Question: Nationalism, Ethnic Conflict, and Self-Determination in the Twentieth Century*, ed. Berch Berberoglu (Philadelphia: Temple University Press, 1995), pp. 38–39.

37. Ibrahim, "The Kurdish National Movement," p. 39.

38. Ibrahim, "The Kurdish National Movement," p. 36. For slightly different estimates of the total Kurdish population, and of Kurds in the various countries in which they are found, see David McDowall, *A Modern History of the Kurds* (London: I. B. Tauris, 1996), pp. 3–4.

39. Bruinessen, *Agha, Shaikh and State*, p. 51.

40. Bruinessen, *Agha, Shaikh and State*, p. 50.

41. Gerard Chaliand, *The Kurdish Tragedy* (London: Zed Books, 1994), p. 19.

42. Bruinessen, *Agha, Shaikh and State*, p. 50.

43. Ibrahim, "The Kurdish National Movement," p. 37.

44. Chaliand, *The Kurdish Tragedy*, pp. 14–15.

45. Kendal, "Kurdistan in Turkey," in *People without a Country: The Kurds and Kurdistan*, ed. Gerard Chaliand (London: Zed Books, 1980), p. 89.

46. Kendal, "Kurdistan in Turkey," pp. 83–87.

47. Bruinessen, *Agha, Shaikh and the State*, pp. 21–22.

48. Bruinessen, *Agha, Shaikh and the State*, p. 37.

49. Ibrahim, "The Kurdish National Movement," pp. 39–40.

50. See the text of relevant sections of the Treaty of Sevres (Articles 62–64) in McDowall, *A Modern History of the Kurds*, pp. 450–51.

51. See Ismet Sheriff Vanly, *Survey of the National Question of Turkish Kurdistan with Historical Background* (Zurich: Hevra, 1971). See also Kemal Kirisci and Gareth M. Winrow, *The Kurdish Question and Turkey: An Example of Trans-State Ethnic Conflict* (London: Frank Cass, 1997).

52. Ibrahim, "The Kurdish National Movement," p. 40.

53. Kendal, "Kurdistan in Turkey," p. 61.

54. See Edmund Ghareeb, *The Kurdish Question in Iraq* (Syracuse, N.Y.: Syracuse University Press, 1981). See also the essays by Ghassemlou, Kendal, Nazdar, and Vanly in Chaliand, *People without a Country*.

55. William Eagleton Jr., *The Kurdish Republic of 1946* (London: Oxford University Press, 1963). See also Farideh Koohi-Kamali, *The Political Development of the Kurds in Iran: Pastoral Nationalism* (London: Palgrave Macmillan, 2004).

56. Ibrahim, "The Kurdish National Movement," p. 41.

57. Bruinessen, *Agha, Shaikh and State*, p. 33.

58. Bruinessen, *Agha, Shaikh and State*, p. 42.

59. David McDowall, *The Kurds: A Nation Denied* (London: Minority Rights Group, 1992), pp. 44–47. See also Ferhad Ibrahim and Gülistan Gürbey, eds., *The Kurdish Conflict in Turkey* (London: Palgrave Macmillan, 2001).

60. McDowall, *The Kurds*, p. 45.

61. Ibrahim, "The Kurdish National Movement," pp. 53–54.

62. Ibrahim, "The Kurdish National Movement," p. 51.

63. McDowall, *The Kurds*, p. 52.

64. Martin Van Bruinessen, "Kurdish Society, Ethnicity, Nationalism and Refugee Problems," in *The Kurds: A Contemporary Overview*, ed. Philip G. Kreyenbroek and Stefan Sperl (London: Routledge, 1992), p. 59.

65. Ibrahim, "The Kurdish National Movement," p. 52.

66. Ibrahim, "The Kurdish National Movement," p. 44.

67. Bruinessen, *Agha, Shaikh and State*, pp. 36–37.

68. "It remains unclear," writes Bruinessen, "to what extent they [the Iraqi KDP] were forced to join the fight against the Iranian Kurds or did so voluntarily. Clearly the Iraqi KDP was highly suspicious of its sister party's contacts with Baghdad." *Agha, Shaikh and State*, p. 39.

69. Bruinessen, *Agha, Shaikh and State*, p. 43.

70. Bruinessen, *Agha, Shaikh and State*, p. 44.

71. Robert Olson, ed., *The Kurdish Nationalist Movement in the 1990s* (Lexington: The University Press of Kentucky, 1996).

Chapter Five

The Rise of Right-Wing Ultranationalist Movements in the Age of Globalization

This chapter examines the relationship between transnational capitalist expansion, decline of national economies, and the rise of right-wing ultranationalist movements around the world. Recent developments in Eastern Europe and the Third World have set the stage for an understanding of similar movements that are now emerging in the United States and other advanced capitalist countries. Examining these developments at some length, I will attempt here to explain the factors that have contributed to the emergence of these movements in the context of economic decline and political reaction in a variety of social settings on a global scale.

Observing the development of nationalism in diverse settings, I will examine a number of national movements that have come to power during the course of the twentieth century. Of special interest here is the emergence of the Nazi movement in Germany, Italian and Spanish fascism, Islamic fundamentalism, Third-World military dictatorships, and contemporary right-wing nationalist movements in the former Yugoslavia and the former Soviet Union, as well as the rise of racist, ultranationalist forces in contemporary mainland Europe, Britain, and the United States, important examples that need to be studied further. This chapter attempts to outline the nature and dynamics of some of these movements and their practices in the context of an analysis of the social, economic, and political transformations that have taken place in the twentieth century. Such an analysis would provide us the broader parameters of socioeconomic and political factors that impact the contemporary world situation and help us explain the dynamics of social change and social transformation that have been taking place in recent decades.

FACTORS CONTRIBUTING TO THE RISE
OF RIGHT-WING ULTRANATIONALIST MOVEMENTS

In an attempt to explain the nature and dynamics of extreme right-wing movements in broad sociological terms, one finds the following conditions that have historically contributed to the rise of nationalism and ultranationalist movements in different societal settings:

(1) Socioeconomic conditions:
  (a) the consolidation of economic power through the concentration and centralization of capital and international capitalist expansion by the transnational monopolies that now operate on a world scale;
  (b) recessions and depressions in the domestic economy, effected by the globalization of capital with the attendant consequences of high unemployment and domestic economic decline;
  (c) growing inequality in income and wealth between different segments of the population, especially between labor and capital at home and abroad;
  (d) decline in the overall standard of living and a rise in the level of poverty on a world scale;
  (e) the contraction of the world economy, including rivalry between the chief economic powers for greater share of the global market.
(2) Sociopolitical conditions:
  (a) the nature of the government in power;
  (b) the level of tolerance and repression by the political regime;
  (c) the world political–military situation, with rivalry between the chief economic powers for territorial expansion;
  (d) the level of political organization and the seriousness of the political threat to the regime in power.

The class nature of the relationship between nationalist movements and the various social classes that support these movements is of crucial importance in the context of the above socioeconomic and political conditions that lead to the rise of extreme right-wing social movements in capitalist society. Here, it is important to delineate the role of various classes in this process—the capitalist class, the petty bourgeoisie, and the working class. Moreover, to understand the dynamics of the relationship between these classes and movements we need to understand the class interests of the social classes involved in this relationship[1]:

(1) The class interests of the capitalist class:
   (a) to maintain order (the capitalist order) through control of the state to facilitate the exploitation of labor for private profit;
   (b) to cultivate relations with petty bourgeois elements and to utilize them in maintaining capitalist rule;
   (c) to use the powers of the state to repress labor or otherwise prevent the working class from coming to power, thus preventing the emergence of socialism.
(2) The class interests of the petty bourgeoisie:
   (a) to safeguard and promote its intermediate class interests;
   (b) to smash the power of big business and the monopolies to carve out a better position for itself under capitalism;
   (c) to smash the power of the working class and the communist movement to prevent the emergence of socialism;
   (d) to advance nationally based small business interests as against those viewed as alien, minority, or belonging to immigrant populations that are seen as threatening local petty bourgeois interests.
(3) The class interests of the working class:
   (a) to fight against capitalist exploitation of labor through strikes and other forms of mass action;
   (b) to fight for the immediate improvement of socioeconomic conditions and increased benefits through trade union activity;
   (c) to fight against the capitalist system through the leadership of a workers party to establish a society ruled by the working class.

The class interests of these classes and the class relations that they entail at various levels of class consciousness are facilitated by domestic economic crisis and a volatile global political–economic situation that give rise to the emergence of various reactionary, ultranationalist movements to safeguard the existing social order.

VARIATIONS IN RIGHT-WING ULTRANATIONALIST MOVEMENTS

There are a variety of right-wing ultranationalist movements in the world today that range from secular nationalist/fascist to religious fundamentalist. Although one can find such movements in many countries across the globe, we focus here on three distinct forms of right-wing radicalism in three different regional settings: (1) those found in the Third World; (2) those that are specific to the advanced capitalist countries; and (3) those that have emerged in Eastern Europe and the former Soviet Union in the aftermath of the collapse of the Soviet bloc. Nationalism takes on a diverse meaning in these three different contexts, and the dynamics of their class leadership and class alliances have thus yielded very different results, depending on the nature and context of the movements that have emerged in these settings.

The Third World

In the Third World, the absence of a viable national bourgeoisie that would lead an anti-imperialist struggle against transnational capital to free itself from neocolonial bondage has led the petty bourgeoisie (especially within the military) to become the leading political force against imperialism.[2] In the absence of a strong workers' movement to take up the leadership of the anti-imperialist nationalist movement, the petty bourgeois forces have come to assume their nationalist role through ironclad dictatorial rule directed not only against foreign capital and its internal neocolonial allies, but also against the working class itself in preventing a worker-led socialist revolution that would put an end to capitalism. Thus, ultranationalist right-wing movements in the Third World came to articulate bourgeois–nationalist ideology under the leadership of the petty bourgeoisie with the intention of smashing both transnational monopoly capital and the working class (communist) movement.

In Turkey, for example, the nationalist movement and the origins of the modern Turkish state go back to the Young Turk Revolution of 1908 led by right-wing ultranationalist (fascist) military officers. Later, after the collapse of the Ottoman Empire, another group of nationalists emerged from within the military to fight against imperialism and maintain internal order in favor of the national and petty bourgeoisies. Rallied behind the nationalist leader Mustafa Kemal, the Kemalists waged a full-scale offensive against the imperialist forces and the internal class forces tied to it. The peasantry was recruited as the natural ally of this nationalist cadre, and it was in this group of independent smallholders that the nationalist leadership found its mass base to defeat imperialism and its internal neocolonial agents.[3]

The petty bourgeois nationalist control of the state in Turkey was a turning point in the consolidation and institutionalization of bourgeois nationalism, which, under the direction of the state, opened the way for independent, national capitalist development. At the same time, the openly repressive nature of the nationalist state toward labor and other progressive sectors of society resulted in the suppression of the people's movement throughout the nationalist period. It was also during this period of right-wing nationalist reaction that the repression of ethnic minorities, including Armenians and Kurds, continued. The ultranationalist violence perpetrated against the Armenians earlier under the Young Turk regime resulted in the first mass genocide of the twentieth century, taking the lives of 1.5 million Armenians.[4] Later, the Kurds faced a similar, though seemingly "less violent" fate intended to wipe out their cultural and national identity (and in effect their very existence), which was accompanied by severe repressive measures, including military pogroms throughout the Kurdish territories in southeastern Turkey.

In Egypt, similar social, economic, and political conditions led to a mass nationalist uprising against the imperialist forces. Supported by a series of revolts of poor peasants and agricultural workers, as well as strikes by industrial workers, the petty bourgeois nationalist forces in the army led by Gamal Abdel Nasser made a successful coup and overthrew the king and the monarchy propped up by British imperialism. The victory of the Free Officers in deposing the monarchy ushered in a period of nationalism and anti-imperialism. As in the case of other nationalist regimes, the Nasser regime rallied the support of broad segments of the masses and used the state as an instrument of national development under petty bourgeois bureaucratic rule.[5] Thus, while the state became the key agent of capital accumulation and the main source of capitalist development that transformed Egypt into an emerging capitalist state, it also became an instrument of mass repression of the working class and other sectors of society that demanded social justice and equitable distribution of the national wealth. Progressive organizations, especially the communists, were subjected to the most severe forms of state repression during this period of right-wing petty bourgeois rule.

In Iraq, a similar dynamic in place led to a nationalist reaction that resulted in the victory of right-wing petty bourgeois forces after independence. Excluded from centers of political and economic power and subordinated to the dictates of the monarchy, the petty bourgeois nationalists came to articulate widespread resentment of foreign control and local ruling-class collaboration with the imperialists. This led to numerous clashes between the colonial state and popular sectors of Iraqi society, including a series of tribal rebellions, labor strikes, mass demonstrations, and clashes between the people and the colonial authorities.[6] The crisis situation emerging from this configuration of social forces led to the emergence of petty bourgeois nationalists who came to lead the national movement against imperialism and its internal neocolonial allies, while at the same time preventing the working class and the popular sectors from exerting influence on the nationalist project. The active role of labor and other progressive organizations among the masses led to large-scale repression of the popular movement once the petty bourgeois nationalist forces came to power. Mass arrests, torture, and execution of communists and other leftists during successive right-wing nationalist regimes became a mainstay of social life in Iraq for decades.

In Iran, the revolution that toppled the shah in 1979 took place under the guise of a mass popular uprising through the use of Islamic ideology directed against foreign capital and its internal neocolonial allies.[7] Led by the mullahs under the direction of Imam Ayatollah Khomeini, the uprising was billed as a religious revolt, hence its characterization as an Islamic revolution. The mass numbers of urban, unemployed, ex-rural peasant migrants thus came to form the political force that the mullahs used, together with the *bazaari* merchants, to collectively challenge the shah's regime.[8]

Focusing on the class nature of the Iranian revolution, it becomes clear, however, that the leadership of the movement that captured power was made up of class forces tied to the big landowners and bazaari merchants allied with them, under the clerical leadership of religious figureheads who were visible in their public criticism of the shah and his regime.[9] Several ayatollahs under the command of Imam Khomeini, as well as a number of civilian leaders such as Bazargan, Bani Sadr, and Ghobzadeh, all paid homage to Islam and the Koran as the leading ideological principle under which they engaged in the making of the revolution. However, notwithstanding their public pronouncements and even personal beliefs in Islam as the guiding light of social change and social transformation, the class character of the Iranian revolution was a product of the social location of the principal actors who led the mass movement.[10]

The fact that the masses of workers and peasants, rich merchants and the unemployed, and students and teachers rallied against the repressive regime of the shah, while several contending groups, ranging from religious fundamentalists to bourgeois liberals to communists and ultraleftists, engaged in struggle over control of the people's movement, when the big landed interests and local merchants succeeded in capturing the organs of state power, testifies to the complexities of the social forces involved in the revolutionary situation.[11] Capturing the reigns of state power and holding on to that power by any means necessary, the landlords and the merchants were able to assert their leadership under the guise of Islam as a mobilizing ideology to prompt the masses into action to serve their own particular (landed and commercial) interests.[12]

While the labor unions in Iran attempted to organize workers along class lines with varying degrees of success (as in the case of the oil workers, who played a pivotal role in the revolution), and while various leftist political parties (such as the Tudeh Party and the Fedayeen) mobilized their supporters to actively engage in political (class) struggle, the broad sections of the masses were more easily mobilized through the use of religious and nationalist ideology, as right-wing fundamentalist forces were better able to manipulate and redirect mass discontent in a religious or nationalist direction, preventing the prevailing class conflicts in Iranian society from becoming open class struggles for state power. Proclaiming to the people that the new state is a state of the masses, the semifeudal/semicapitalist theocratic state of the landlords and the clergy maintained tight control over the peasantry and the unemployed sections of the working class, advancing their own (landlord–clergy) interests as those of the people, sanctioned by Allah, the almighty, to whom they paid official homage by invoking the principles of Islam.[13]

The reality of the situation in Iran was much different, however, than the official propaganda of the Islamic state would have it. The state ushered in by the revolutionary forces in February 1979 was not a religious one at all. It was Islamic in name only, and only to the degree that some key clergy, with full religious credentials, were presented as spokespersons for the new state, legitimized by their repeated appearances on radio, television, and in print media. Behind the scenes, however (in the national assembly, in the supreme organs of the state, down to the various local bodies of state organizations), the situation was quite different: Business and business-oriented transactions of a semifeudal and capitalist nature, not the Koran, were the motive force of public policy bent on profiting the key beneficiaries of the new authoritarian state.[14] Thus, the imposition of a theocratic dictatorship over the masses was less for its theocratic character than its dictatorial nature in a new alliance of neocolonial forces negotiating the terms of its dependence on one or another of its more advanced capitalist–imperialist senior partners dominating the world economy.[15]

The fact that the landlords and the *bazaari* merchants captured state power with the aid of the Islamic clergy explains well why Islam could so easily come to serve the interests of these classes in legitimizing their rule. What is not so clear, however, is how it is that the forces that came to power more than two decades ago have managed to stay in power despite the autocratic nature of their rule. It is here, then, that the role of religion as a legitimizing ideology can explain the power of religious phenomena in interacting with politics and the state to maintain class domination in society.[16]

Clearly, the dominant forces in charge of the sociopolitical situation are aware of their power and rule over society and have done much to maintain their control of the state. What is less clear, however, is the longevity of their rule, especially given the restrictive and authoritarian nature of their reign over society. This, too, can be explained through an analysis of class relations, for ideological control emanates from the ruling class's control over the major institutions of society. Thus, in Iran after the revolution, the ideas of the Islamic clergy, as reflective of those of the landlords and the merchants, became the generalized ideas disseminated through the schools, the media, and other organs of state power that came to serve as the dominant ruling ideology.[17] In this sense, Islam has been able to buy time for itself and for its class masters in serving as the ideology of the new ruling class, hence serving a similar function as nationalism in mobilizing the masses behind the banner of a "religious" revolution. Thus, religion became an important ideological tool in the hands of the social forces intent on winning the support of the masses in their drive to take state power. And it is in this way that the organic link between religion and nationalism was established and used to effect a mass, anti-imperialist revolution that overthrew the shah's regime in Iran.

Although variations exist in factors determining the nature and outcome of a specific Third-World nationalist movement (such as the influence of religious and cultural factors most visible in fundamentalist movements, as in Iran and Algeria), one can delineate the class forces leading these movements by focusing on their social base and the internal structure of their main organizations. In this way, one can be better able to understand the nature and dynamics of right-wing ultranationalist movements and their political agenda to effect change in line with their class interests.

The Advanced Capitalist Countries

There have been a number of right-wing ultranationalist movements in advanced capitalist countries throughout the course of the twentieth century. The most extreme and well-known case is that of Nazism in Germany in the mid-twentieth century. While other forms of ultranationalist movements exist in Europe, the United States, and other advanced capitalist regions of the world, such as Italian fascism, Spanish Francoism, and the U.S. Ku Klux Klan, German Nazism has been the most violent and brutal form of extreme nationalism, leading to the calculated mass murder of millions of people in a few short years.

The Nazi movement was heavily financed by German monopoly capitalists. Big business in Germany used the Jewish threat to control and repress the working class through the use of the Nazi movement to safeguard capitalist interests and maintain the capitalist order at a time of great economic crisis.[18] The fact that Germany had plunged into a severe depression and that an extreme ultranationalist movement could divert the frustrations of the working class away from capital and toward an ethnic group characterized as a rival force, helped consolidate the Nazi ultranationalist program that German big business promoted as a way out of the capitalist crisis.[19] The growing power of the working class and the electoral gains of the communist party showed the urgency of smashing the power of labor to prevent a socialist revolution during the German great depression. In this case, Nazism served as a source of social control and prolongation of the existing capitalist order through repression in its most brutal form. Hence, in Germany (as in Italy) fascism became monopoly capital's answer to the threat of socialism, when the working class had come very close to overthrowing the capitalist state.[20]

Today, conditions that in the past led to the emergence of extreme right-wing nationalist movements are developing rapidly throughout the advanced capitalist countries. In Germany, France, Italy, and Britain these movements have begun to resurface under a neo-Nazi banner, targeting immigrant groups and people of Asian, Middle Eastern, and North African origin.[21] Violent fascist gangs are terrorizing and killing their chosen opponents without fear of police intervention. These groups and others like them have become the shock troops of monopoly capital in decline, desperately seeking and utilizing right-wing extremist forces to dampen popular resistance to its rule in a last-ditch effort to stay in power.

In Germany, anti-immigrant racist attacks by neo-Nazi groups have been directed against Turkish "guest" workers who constitute a good part of the low-paid industrial work force that has been flowing into the country over the past few decades. Their distinct cultural practices and social standing in segregated immigrant neighborhoods have turned them into easy targets for disaffected German youth organized into right-wing racist gangs affiliated with neo-Nazi groups that fuel such antiforeign ultranationalist propaganda and violence that have resulted in burning of homes and cold-blooded murder in incidents across Germany in recent years.[22]

In Britain, the targets of antiforeign racist attacks are East Indian, African, Middle Eastern, and Caribbean immigrants. Occupying the lowest levels of the industrial and service sectors and found in many of the menial jobs mainly concentrated in London and surrounding cities, these clearly identifiable immigrants are often victims of gang violence perpetrated by skinheads and other racist groups promoted by ultranationalist fascist cults like the National Front.[23] These groups, while having their own rightist agenda, perform a key function in preserving existing capitalist relations by misdirecting the anger and hostility of the British working class against immigrant workers in racist terms. Weakening the unity of the working class through such "divide and conquer" tactics propagated in ultranationalist language, the powerful interests that support and finance such efforts are clearly the beneficiaries of the violence perpetrated against the communities who pay a heavy price for their very right to exist.

In France and Italy, right-wing anti-immigrant attacks have been directed against North Africans and people of Middle Eastern origin. Cities like Paris, Marseilles, Rome, Milan, and Naples have become hotbeds of right-wing fascist activity directed against Algerians, Moroccans, Tunisians, Libyans, and

Albanians who have immigrated to France and Italy in search of better jobs and a better life for their families.[24] These previously colonized peoples are now resented by ultranationalist groups in the typical racist mode of colonial thinking that characterize them in culturally and socially inferior terms. Right-wing political parties backed by big business have fanned the flames of racist violence directed against these immigrants to confuse the working class and middle sectors of society and cultivate a fascist movement to keep the labor movement in check. As the blame for the continuing economic crisis in these countries is placed on immigrants, the violence perpetrated against them has become institutionalized and justified by a variety of extremist groups operating as street gangs in pursuit of immigrant families.

In the United States, right-wing ultranationalist groups are becoming more and more visible. The decline of the U.S. economy over the past two decades has brought about a lowering of the living standards of the U.S. working class, and this has led to resentment against immigrants who are blamed for taking away American jobs. Although higher rates of unemployment are the result of plant closings and the corporate move to low-wage Third-World countries, such as Mexico, the capitalist media has exploited the racial divide by fueling racist propaganda against immigrant groups, blaming them for the ills of society.[25] While this has served to divide people and thus prevent the development of a strong labor movement, the working class is becoming more and more aware of the situation and of its central role in the fight against the forces of reaction that are behind the right-wing agenda. Hence, it is in this sense that the rise of right-wing movements in the United States in recent years is a reflection of the crisis of monopoly capitalism in this final stage of imperialist expansion. However, with the growing people's movements in both the advanced capitalist countries and the Third World, broad segments of the working class and its allies are beginning to forge a popular coalition of forces to fight the right-wing reaction and halt the racist agenda fostered by big business.

Eastern Europe and the Former Soviet Union

In Eastern Europe and the former Soviet Union, most notably in the former Yugoslavia, the reactionary nationalist forces that had been hiding behind the thin veil of state socialism took advantage of the opening accorded by the changes in East Europe to impose an openly right-wing bourgeois dictatorship, first in Slovenia and Croatia, and later in other parts of the former Yugoslavia—most violently in Bosnia-Herzegovina.[26] A similar process of state control in the hands of bourgeois and petty bourgeois officials in other provinces, including Serbia, led to a destructive confrontation between rival nationalist forces in post-socialist Yugoslavia.

A situation similar to this has also been developing elsewhere in Eastern Europe and in the newly independent republics of the former Soviet Union. In Romania and Bulgaria, right-wing anticommunist elements that came to power after the collapse of the Caucescu and Zhivkov regimes have through a succession of bourgeois governments consolidated their hold over the state. In Poland and Hungary, the movements that brought to power anticommunist bourgeois elements in the late 1980s have likewise strengthened the hands of right-wing forces in the struggle for control of the state.[27]

In Poland, the failure of liberal reforms under the Lech Walesa regime led to the growth not only of a leftist opposition, but also a rightist, ultranationalist movement. In the Czech Republic, the bourgeois anticommunist leadership that came to power under Vaclav Havel in the aftermath of the collapse of the communist state in Czechoslovakia set the stage for right-wing anticommunist elements to freely operate throughout the country.[28]

In East Germany, neo-Nazi groups have sprung up and spread to many cities. High levels of unemployment and social deprivation throughout the former GDR have brought misery to millions and forced them into destitution. The devastating economic situation experienced by millions of Germans in the East has led to resentment on both sides of the new united Germany. The move toward privatization and the transition to a market economy have generated a new set of contradictions that are beginning to surface in the eastern half of the country.[29]

The appeal to national symbols under an ultranationalist banner has led to the mobilization of right-wing extremist groups from Poland to Russia, from the Baltic states to the Transcaucasian republics.[30] The right-wing bourgeois forces that have come to play a central role in maintaining power in these and other newly independent republics have strengthened the hands of ultranationalist groups on the extreme right—a situation that has further inflamed ethnic passions, as in Chechnya and Nagorno-Karabagh. The war between Armenia and Azerbaijan, for example, has led to further destabilization of the entire Transcaucasian region. Moreover, the strengthening of religious and cultural ties between Azerbaijan and Turkey has led to increased tensions between Armenia and Turkey regarding Turkish intentions toward Armenia, given the continued discord between the two countries that is historic in nature.[31]

The economic crisis that these countries have been facing in the post-Soviet period has been the primary instigator for the emergence of extreme nationalist movements. As the collapse of the newly established market economies in these former socialist states has resulted in mass unemployment, poverty, and destitution among large segments of the population, the reactionary bourgeois forces are attempting to consolidate their power and impose repressive authoritarian rule over the population to maintain control. And in this context, various minority ethnic populations have been used as scapegoats to channel the anger and frustration of the masses in a right-wing, racist/ethnonationalist direction to prevent a popular uprising against the system.[32]

CONCLUSION

If these competing ultraconservative, right-wing nationalist movements represent different forms of repressive authoritarian rule in the classic sense (one applying to the case of the advanced capitalist countries, another to that of the Third World, and yet a third, modified version in the postsocialist states), how then is one to explain the reemergence of the radical right in Europe (directed primarily against immigrants) in the Third World (under the guise of Islamic fundamentalism), and in Eastern Europe and the Balkans (in the form of ethnic conflict)? What are the class forces behind these movements and what are their social agendas? What are their nature, origins, dynamics, and contradictions? What are the danger signs and the implications of their coming to power in this period of economic crisis and decline? What are the parallels between contemporary developments and what we have experienced in the not too distant past following the great depression?

An analysis of the social context of the emergence and development of these movements and their dynamics would go a long way in helping us understand the contending class forces and class struggles in society that will eventually lead to the resolution of these contradictions. It would also provide us some tentative answers to these important questions and hence delineate the nature and types of right-wing ultranationalist movements that have come to play a significant role in the world today.

NOTES

1. For an extended discussion on the nature and interests of various classes in capitalist society, see Berch Berberoglu, *Class Structure and Social Transformation* (Westport, Conn.: Praeger 1994). See also Albert J. Szymanski, *Class Structure: A Critical Perspective* (Westport, Conn.: Praeger, 1983).

2. See Albert J. Szymanski, *The Logic of Imperialism* (New York: Praeger, 1981).

3. Berch Berberoglu, "Nationalism and Ethnic Rivalry in the Early Twentieth Century," *Nature, Society, and Thought* 4, no. 3 (1991): 269–301.

4. Vahakn N. Dadrian, *The History of the Armenian Genocide: Ethnic Conflict from the Balkans to Anatolia to the Caucasus* (Providence, R.I.: Berghahn, 1995).

5. For an analysis of Egypt under Nasser as a nationalist state–capitalist society, see Mahmoud Hussein, *Class Conflict in Egypt: 1945–1970* (New York: Monthly Review Press, 1973).

6. Joe Stork, "Class, State, and Politics in Iraq," in *Power and Stability in the Middle East*, ed. Berch Berberoglu (London: Zed Books, 1989), pp. 31–54.

7. Fred Halliday, *Iran: Dictatorship and Development* (New York: Penguin, 1979).

8. Farideh Farhi, "Class Struggles, the State, and Revolution in Iran," in *Power and Stability in the Middle East*, ed. Berberoglu, pp. 90–113.

9. Halliday, *Iran: Dictatorship and Development*; A. Ashraf, "Bazaar and Mosque in Iran's Revolution," *MERIP Reports* 13, no. 3 (March–April 1983); Farhi, "Class Struggles, the State, and Revolution in Iran."

10. Here it should be emphasized that while the ideology of the principal actors leading the revolution serves to define the nature and content of the revolution and the postrevolutionary state, the character of the new state and the class interests it comes to serve are very much dependent on the policies of the new state—policies from which various sectors of the population either benefit or lose.

11. See John Foran, *Fragile Resistance: Social Transformation in Iran from 1500 to the Revolution* (Boulder, Colo.: Westview, 1993) and "The Iranian Revolution of 1977–79: A Challenge for Social Theory," in *A Century of Revolution: Social Movements in Iran*, ed. John Foran (Minneapolis: University of Minnesota Press, 1994); M. Parsa, *The Social Origins of the Iranian Revolution* (New Brunswick, N.J.: Rutgers University Press, 1989); Valentine Moghadam, "Populist Revolution and the Islamic State in Iran," in *Revolution in the World System*, ed. Terry Boswell (Westport, Conn.: Greenwood, 1989) and "Islamic Populism, Class, and Gender in Postrevolutionary Iran," in Foran, *A Century of Revolution*.

12. Ashraf, "Bazaar and Mosque in Iran's Revolution"; S. Bakhash, *The Reign of the Ayatollahs* (New York: Basic, 1983).

13. Bakhash, *The Reign of the Ayatollahs*; Ashraf, "Bazaar and Mosque in Iran's Revolution"; N. Keddie, *Iran: Religion, Politics, and Society* (London: Frank Cass, 1980).

14. Farhi, "Class Struggles, the State, and Revolution in Iran"; N. Keddie and Eric Hooglund, eds., *The Iranian Revolution and the Islamic Republic* (Washington, D.C.: Middle East Institute, 1982).

15. M. H. Pesaran, "The System of Dependent Capitalism in Pre- and Post-Revolutionary Iran," *International Journal of Middle East Studies* 14 (1982); M. Zavareei, "Dependent Capitalist Development in Iran and the Mass Uprising of 1979," *Research in Political Economy* 5 (1982). While the Islamic forces that waged battle against the shah's regime and came to power were characterized as anti-West due to their anti-U.S. stance given the U.S. historic role in Iran and its support of the shah's regime, the new Islamic state was quick to reveal its true class character by its realliance with some of the key European states to advance the semifeudal/semicapitalist interests of its new ruling classes.

16. Mansoor Moaddel, in emphasizing the role of ideology in the Iranian Revolution, gives primacy to the ideological factor as the driving force of social change that

affects the dynamics of class relations and class struggle against the state challenged by the oppositional ideology within the context of what he calls "a particular historical episode." See M. Moaddel, "Ideology as Episodic Discourse: The Case of the Iranian Revolution," *American Sociological Review* 57 (June 1992): 359; M. Moaddel, *Class, Politics, and Ideology in the Iranian Revolution* (New York: Columbia University Press, 1993), pp. 15–16. While this notion goes against Marxist formulations of the role of ideology as superstructural phenomena that are a reflection of class interests, Moaddel's analysis does, however, highlight the importance of ideology in political struggles for state power.

17. Keddie, *Iran: Religion, Politics, and Society*; Farhi, "Class Struggles, the State, and Revolution in Iran."

18. See Franz L. Neumann, *Behemoth: The Structure and Practice of National Socialism, 1933–1944* (New York: Harper & Row, 1944). See also Daniel Guerin, *Fascism and Big Business* (New York: Monad Press, 1945).

19. Arthur Schweitzer, *Big Business and the Third Reich* (Bloomington: Indiana University Press, 1964). See also James Pool and Suzanne Pool, *Who Financed Hitler: The Secret Funding of Hitler's Rise to Power, 1919–1933* (New York: Dial Press, 1978).

20. Guerin, *Fascism and Big Business*. See also Albert J. Szymanski, *The Capitalist State and the Politics of Class* (Cambridge, Mass.: Winthrop Publishers, 1978).

21. Piero Ignazi, *Extreme Right Parties in Western Europe* (Oxford, U.K.: Oxford University Press, 2003).

22. Alana Lentin, *Racism and Anti-Racism in Europe* (London: Pluto Press, 2004).

23. Lentin, *Racism and Anti-Racism in Europe*.

24. Ignazi, *Extreme Right Parties in Western Europe*.

25. For an analysis of the economic roots of racism, see Peter Knapp and Alan J. Spector, *Crisis and Change* (Chicago: Nelson-Hall Publishers, 1991).

26. Jasminka Udovicki, "Nationalism, Ethnic Conflict, and Self-Determination in the Former Yugoslavia," in *The National Question: Nationalism, Ethnic Conflict, and Self-Determination in the Twentieth Century*, ed. Berch Berberoglu (Philadelphia: Temple University Press, 1995), chap. 12. See also Aleksandar Pavkovic, *The Fragmentation of Yugoslavia: Nationalism and War in the Balkans* (Hampshire, U.K.: Palgrave Macmillan, 2000); Dusan Kecmanovic, *Ethnic Times: Exploring Ethnonationalism in the Former Yugoslavia* (Westport, Conn.: Praeger, 2001); Cathie Carmichael, *Ethnic Cleansing in the Balkans: Nationalism and the Destruction of Tradition* (New York: Routledge, 2002); David Chandler, *Bosnia: Faking Democracy after Dayton* (London: Pluto Press, 2000).

27. Jan Adam, *The Social Costs of Transformation in Post-Socialist Countries: The Cases of Poland, the Czech Republic and Hungary* (New York: Palgrave, 2000).

28. Adam, *The Social Costs of Transformation in Post-Socialist Countries*.

29. Laszlo Andor and Martin Summers, *Market Failure: A Guide to the East European "Economic Miracle"* (London: Pluto Press, 1998).

30. Suzanne Goldenberg, *The Pride of Small Nations: The Caucasus and Post-Soviet Disorder* (London: Zed Books, 1994); Mark R. Beissinger, *Nationalist Mobi-*

lization and the Collapse of the Soviet State (Cambridge, U.K.: Cambridge University Press, 2002).

31. I refer here to the Armenian genocide of 1915—an event that is of utmost historic importance to the Armenian collective memory. See Dadrian, *The History of the Armenian Genocide*.

32. These include the repression of Chechnians in Russia and discrimination against the Hungarians in Romania, as well as mistreatment of gypsies (Roma) in Slovakia and elsewhere in Eastern Europe, and various other minority ethnic groups in Eastern Europe and the former Soviet Union.

Part Three

NATIONALISM, THE STATE, AND CLASS STRUGGLE

Chapter Six

Class, State, and Nation: The Pillars of Nationalism and Ethnic Conflict

The relationship between class, state, and nation is a central one that defines the nature and dynamics of nationalism and ethnic conflict. This was addressed both in the early theoretical chapters and subsequently in the various cases discussed in this book. Here, I provide a critical analysis of this important relationship and examine its political implications at greater length.

While class, state, and nation are the quintessential pillars of nationalism and ethnic conflict, it is the political dynamics of this triangular relationship that gives nationalism its ideological expression. Thus, I argue that the class nature of nationalism and ethnic conflict becomes evident when ethnonational struggles are placed in their proper historical and sociopolitical context. Moreover, this dynamic operates at both the national and international levels and is the result of a complex set of relations that are class determined.

Nationalism and ethnic conflict are, therefore, in a very fundamental way the outcomes of a process wherein various competing class forces have a particular relationship to the state. And this relationship is inherently political in nature and takes place within the context of a nation-state. Given this reality, it is of utmost importance to study the nature and dynamics of the nation-state and the process by which vested interests within the nation-state have a stake in promoting nationalism and ethnic conflict in order to advance their particular class interests.

THE CLASS NATURE OF NATION AND NATIONALISM

"What is the relationship between the division of society into classes and into nations?" asks G. Glezerman, "Is there a link between class and national relations and if there is what is its nature?"[1]

It has been my contention throughout this book that the phenomena of nation and nationalism cannot be fully understood without an analysis of their class nature and dynamics. Class relations and class struggle are central to the dynamics and contradictions of class society, above all to the structure and operation of the state and the nature and composition of the nation and society in general, as well as their transformation.

"The formation of nations," writes Glezerman, "always has a definite socio-economic content."[2] Although a nation encompasses all classes, not all classes play a similar role in the formation of a nation. What is crucial, Glezerman points out, is to distinguish the leading (ruling) class that puts its mark on the nation and determines its social, economic, political, and ideological course of development.

> In the first place it is a class which embodies the mode of production that forms the foundation for the community of economic life emerging in a nation. In the second place, this class is the hegemon in the struggle for the realization of the historical tasks on which the development and the future of the nation depend. In the third place, it plays the decisive role in defining the socio-economic image of a nation and its relations with other nations.[3]

Thus, Glezerman continues:

> The formation of nations, for example, in Western Europe, North America and elsewhere was closely connected with the growth of capitalist relations. And since this took place on the basis of the development of the capitalist mode of production, the rise of national links was in effect . . . a process of the creation of bourgeois links. Consequently, the national state which took shape under these circumstances was a bourgeois state.[4]

Clearly, as Glezerman points out, the history of the bourgeois state is the history of capitalism and the capitalist class. The fact that the emergence and development of capitalism has coincided with the development of the capitalist state over the course of European history and the history of other regions where capitalism has made headway attests to the relationship between the two, which is more than coincidental—it is the outcome of class interest and class intent. This is true with similar developments in nations that have embarked on (or are in the process of embarking on) capitalism and capitalist relations elsewhere in the world, historically and today.

In this context, I argue that the dominant class in capitalist society controls the state and dictates its terms over society to serve its own narrow class interests (and does so through its social, economic, political, and ideological hegemony), and that the contradictions imbedded in capitalist society facilitate the development of class conflict and class struggle that brings to the forefront the class nature of society and the nation. Hence, while "national consolidation became an essential factor in the formation of bourgeois nations," Glezerman reminds us, "the further development and intensification of the class struggle brings the contrast between classes into the forefront."[5]

This view further reinforces my argument that the political, ideological, cultural, and other superstructural manifestations of class can only be clearly understood through an analysis of the structure and contradictions of class relations and class struggle as rooted in historically specific, social–economic conditions of society.

The point being stressed here is that an analysis of property-based unequal social relations in the organization of material production is the key to an understanding of the nature of class divisions in society. The social location of people in the production process, situated according to their relation to the ownership/control of the means of production, is the decisive element that defines class relations. And it is from these historically specific social relations of production that inequalities arise, leading to class conflict and class struggles—that is, struggles for state power.

"Is there any reason to be surprised," Marx asks, "that a society based on class conflict leads to brutal opposition, and in the last resort to a clash between individuals?"[6] "An oppressed class," he writes, "is the condition of existence of every society based on class conflict. Thus the liberation of the oppressed class necessarily involves the creation of a new society."[7]

Under capitalism, the dominant capitalist class, through its control of the major superstructural institutions, obtains political control and disseminates capitalist ideology, hence assuring its ideological hegemony over society. An aspect of this ideological control that promotes the interests of the bourgeoisie at the superstructural level is bourgeois nationalism—an ideology propped up by the capitalist class to promote national and ethnic distinctions and divisions in order to prevent the development of class consciousness among workers and to neutralize their frustration against the system by channeling mass discontent toward other nations and ethnic groups.

"The bourgeoisie and its nationalist parties," writes Glezerman, attempt "to impose a 'unified' national ideology upon the proletariat":

> They preach class peace within a nation in order to cover up class antagonism with a national banner and prevent the proletarians from coalescing into a class. Bourgeois ideologues incite mistrust and hatred for "alien" nations so as to strengthen the "unity" of their own nation.[8]

"Many bourgeois sociologists and reformists regard national interests as a sort of 'neutral' ground on which all classes unite," Glezerman continues; "This conception has nothing in common with reality":

> It tears national interests away from class interests in order to hide or smooth over the contradictions between the interests of the opposing classes in a given nation and, at the same time, to place proletarians of different nations in opposition to each other.[9]

Thus, "many bourgeois sociologists attach primary importance to the struggle of races and nations," Glezerman concludes, "in order to slur over the contradictions between the interests of the proletariat and the bourgeoisie."[10] This is done with the attempt to "dampen the class struggle and replace it with a struggle against 'alien' nations."[11]

While this process has served to block the development of class consciousness among workers, thus hampering the prospects for social revolution, the material conditions of life under capitalism, however, eventually force workers to organize and rise up against the prevailing exploitative system. As the working class becomes class conscious and discovers that its social condition is more and more the result of its exploitation by the capitalists, it invariably begins to organize and fight back to secure for itself economic benefits and political rights that it is generally denied in capitalist society.

The exploitation of labor and the domination of the working class by capital eventually leads to class struggle, and ultimately to the struggle for state power: "The conflict between proletariat and bourgeoisie," Marx and Engels remind us, "is a struggle of one class against another, a struggle that means in its highest expression a total revolution."[12]

It is in this context of the centrality of class and class struggle in capitalist society that we find the state as a decisive political force that assumes the task of determining the boundaries of the nation and establishing the parameters of national politics that are driven by the logic of class relations and class struggle under capitalism.

CLASS AND STATE:
THE CLASS NATURE OF POLITICS AND THE STATE

Central to the study of the state and its role in society is an analysis of the class nature of politics and the state, as well as the linkage between class and state. Taken together, these constitute the very social foundations of the state as the central political institution of modern society.

"We began really to understand the nature of the state and the nation, and their transformations," writes M. Adler, "only when the mysterious power of the state, apparently based upon the will of the whole people, was revealed as the organized will to power of one class over the other, and when its source was disclosed in the economic opposition of class interests."[13] "This could only be understood," Adler continues, "when the cosy picture of the unity of the nation was dissolved into that of a class struggle within the people that permeated every stage in the historical development of the state."[14]

The central question regarding the nature of the state is the character of its relationship with the prevailing social classes in society. In this regard, class structure and class relations are the major determinants of politics and the state, and class conflicts and class struggles lie at the center of social and political transformations, for it is only through such struggles that state power is attained. Political power is a manifestation of economic power driven by money and wealth. To maintain and secure its dominant position in society, the ruling class controls the state and other political institutions of society in order to hold down the masses and to perpetuate their continued exploitation and oppression.

The emergence of the state, as the chief superstructural institution of society to protect the interests of the dominant ruling class, coincided with the emergence of social classes and class struggles. A direct product of the social–economic base, the state, once captured by the newly emergent dominant class, became an instrument of force to maintain the rule of wealth and privilege against the laboring masses, that is, to maintain economic and political domination by the few over the many.

The political power vested in the state by the dominant ruling class was to keep the subordinate classes in check. Thus, the state

> would not only safeguard the newly-acquired property of private individuals . . . , would not only sanctify private property, formerly held in such light esteem, and pronounce this sanctification the highest purpose of human society, . . . but also the right of the possessing class to exploit the non-possessing classes and the rule of the former over the latter.[15]

The translation of economic wealth into political power in the hands of the dominant class to hold down the exploited masses was clearly pointed out by Engels in his book *The Origin of the Family, Private Property, and the State*, where he writes:

> it is, as a rule, the state of the most powerful, economically dominant class, which, through the medium of the state, becomes also the politically dominant class, and thus acquires new means of holding down and exploiting the oppressed class. Thus, the state of antiquity was above all the state of the slave owners for the purpose of holding down the slaves, as the feudal state was the organ of the nobility for holding down the peasant serfs and bondsmen, and the modern representative state is an instrument of exploitation of wage labor by capital.[16]

Hence, in all class-divided societies throughout history, write Marx and Engels, "political power is merely the organized power of one class for oppressing another."[17]

In his classic work *The State and Revolution*, Lenin clearly and concisely reminds us that in all class-divided societies the *class essence* of the state's rule over society is rooted in domination and exploitation by a propertied ruling class of the propertyless, oppressed class. In our epoch, writes Lenin,

> Every state in which private ownership of the land and means of production exists, in which capital dominates, however democratic it may be, is a capitalist state, a machine used by the capitalists to keep the working class and the poor peasants in subjection.[18]

In capitalist society, the state, reflecting the interests of the dominant capitalist class, can thus be characterized as the *capitalist state*, for this state is nothing less than a political organ of the bourgeoisie to safeguard its property-based interests. Thus, "the more it [the state] becomes the organ of a particular class, the more it directly enforces the supremacy of that class."[19] In this context, Marx and Engels point out that "the bourgeoisie has . . . conquered for itself, in the modern representative State, exclusive political sway. The executive of the modern State is but a committee for managing the common affairs of the whole bourgeoisie."[20]

In his book *What Does the Ruling Class Do When It Rules?* Goran Therborn argues that "different types of class relations and of class power generate corresponding forms of state organization" and explains how "the class character of the state apparatus is determined and revealed"[21]:

> Class and state condition each other: where there are no classes, there is no state. In class societies, moreover, social relations are first and foremost class relations. Thus, by definition, every state has a class character, and every class society has a ruling class (or bloc of ruling classes).[22]

Central to Therborn's analysis of the relationship of the economic base to the political superstructure is the role of the *class struggle* engendered by the dominant mode of production. "In very general terms," writes Therborn,

> the character of state power is defined by the two fundamental processes of determination of the superstructure by the base—processes which in reality are two aspects of the same determination. One of these is the systemic logic of social modes of production, that is to say, the tendencies and contradictions of the specific dynamic of each mode. The other is the struggle of classes, defined by their position in the mode of production.[23]

In this formulation, the state is actively involved in the reproduction of the dominant relations of production: "Invariably the state enters into the reproduction of the relations of production by providing the latter with a stabilizing legal framework backed by force."[24] And in so doing, the state reinforces the legal boundaries that define relations between dominant and subordinate classes.[25]

According to Therborn's argument, then, "the economic base determines the political superstructure by entering into the reproduction of state power and the state apparatus" and "shapes the character of state power by, among other things, providing the basic parameters of state action."[26] Further, because "exploitative relations of production need a repressive political apparatus as their ultimate guarantee,"[27] the state comes to assume this role to "promote and defend the ruling class and its mode of exploitation or supremacy."[28] Thus, "the ruling class exercises its ruling power over other classes and strata through the state—through holding state power."[29]

Albert Szymanski, in his book *The Capitalist State and the Politics of Class*, makes a similar case in favor of this approach by stressing the fact that the state plays a central role in society and that this has immense political implications. Examining the nature and role of the state in class society in general and capitalist society in particular, Szymanski writes:

> The state is an instrument by which the exploitation of the economically subordinate class is secured by the economically dominant class that controls the state. . . . The social relationships and the social order that the state guarantees are thus the social relationships of inequality and the order of property and exploitation. . . .
>
> The state in capitalist society is a capitalist state by virtue of its domination by the capitalist class and in that it functions most immediately in the interests of capital.[30]

Moreover, under capitalism the state must function within the confines of an economic, military, political, and ideological environment structured by capitalist relations of production.[31] This means that the logic of capitalist economic relations, reinforced by capital's ideological hegemony, dictate the policies the state must follow, which are formulated within a very limited range of options allowed by the capitalist mode of production. Thus the state in capitalist society is controlled by the capitalist class through both direct and indirect mechanisms that foster the interests of this class. However, while the state "is normally under the domination of the class that owns and controls the means of production," adds Szymanski, "the ruling class must take into account both the demands and likely responses of other classes when it makes state policy. If it does not, it may suffer very serious consequences, including social revolution."[32]

As the ruling capitalist class continues its sway over the state, the class struggle waged against this state more and more takes on a political character. As a result, "The fight of the oppressed class against the ruling class becomes necessarily a political fight, a fight first of all against the political dominance of this class."[33] The centrality of the state as an instrument of *class rule*, therefore, assumes an added importance, for political power contested by the warring classes takes on its real meaning in securing the rule of the victorious class when that power is ultimately exercised through the instrumentality of the state.

Historically, since the end of the nineteenth century, the state in advanced capitalist societies has developed parallel to the development and expansion of the capitalist economy in its transition to the higher, monopoly stage. Within this process of the state's development from early to mature capitalism, the structural imperatives of capital accumulation placed the state in the service of capital, thus transforming it into a *capitalist state*.

The development of capitalism over the past one hundred years formed and transformed the capitalist state into its modern, contemporary stage. In line with its functions in facilitating the existing mode of production and its attendant superstructure, the political apparatus of modern capitalism has come to reflect the changing structure of the capitalist economy, which increasingly operates on a world scale.

With the globalization of capital, the capitalist state has come to assume a greater responsibility in organizing and leading the global capitalist system, thus adopting the role of an imperial state charged with the control and rationalization of the new international division of labor. It is within this context of the globalization of the advanced capitalist superstructure that the crisis of the capitalist state manifests itself on a world scale.[34]

The crisis of the advanced capitalist state on the world scene is a manifestation of the contradictions of the world economy, which in the late twentieth century reached a critical stage in its development. In the current phase of the crisis of the capitalist state, the critical problems that the state faces are of such magnitude that they threaten the very existence of the world capitalist system as a global power bloc. The growing prospects of inter-imperialist rivalry between the major capitalist powers, backed up by their states, are effecting changes in their relations that render the world political economy a more and more unstable character. The rivalry between the major capitalist powers, which is not always restricted to the economic field but has political (and even military) implications, is global in magnitude.

While the contradictions and conflicts imbedded in relations between the rival states of the major capitalist powers will continue to be an important component of international relations in the early twenty-first century, the most critical problem facing the advanced capitalist state, however, is the crisis emanating from the restructuring of the international division of labor involving the transfer of the production process to overseas territories, in line with the globalization of capital on a world scale.[35]

CLASS, POWER, AND IDEOLOGICAL HEGEMONY: NATIONALISM AND THE POLITICAL RULE OF THE BOURGEOISIE

In explaining the process by which the capitalist class controls the state and secures its dominance in society one must turn to an analysis of bourgeois cultural and ideological hegemony. The relationship of the (political–ideological) superstructure to its (social–economic) class base, which allows control of the major superstructural institutions of society by the dominant ruling class, reveals the nature of the dominant ideas prevalent in that society. And the state, as the supreme political organ whose legitimacy is institutionalized by law, plays a key role in the dissemination of these ideas, thus ensuring the ideological hegemony of the ruling class.

In maintaining its power over society, it is not enough for the ruling class simply to take control of the state machine and rule society directly through force and coercion; it must also convince the oppressed classes of the legitimacy of its rule. Hence, as Antonio Gramsci has pointed out, "The state is the entire complex of practical and theoretical activities with which the ruling class not only justifies and maintains its dominance, but manages to win the active consent of those over whom it rules."[36]

Through its dominance of the political and ideological institutions of society, the ruling class is thus able to control and shape the ideas, hence consciousness, of the masses. With the acceptance of its ideas and the legitimization of its rule, the ruling class is able to exercise control and domination of society through its ideological hegemony at the level of the superstructure, and this is done with the assistance and instrumentality of the state.

Louis Althusser, in his seminal essay "Ideology and Ideological State Apparatuses," has pointed out that central to the process of ruling-class ideological domination is the installation by the ruling class of the dominant ideology in the ideological state apparatuses.[37] "The ideology of the ruling class," Althusser argues, "does not become the ruling ideology by virtue of the seizure of state power alone. It is by the installation of the ideological state apparatuses in which this ideology is realized itself that it becomes the ruling ideology."[38]

The relationship between ruling-class domination and the dominant ideology also has been emphasized by Nicos Poulantzas, who further developed Althusser's conceptualization of ideology, situating it in the context of class domination and class struggle. "The dominant ideology, by assuring the practical insertion of agents in the social structure," Poulantzas points out, "aims at the maintenance (the cohesion) of the structure, and this means above all class domination and exploitation."[39]

> It is precisely in this way that within a social formation ideology is dominated by the ensemble of representations, values, notions, beliefs, etc. by means of which class domination is perpetuated: in other words it is dominated by what can be called the ideology of the dominant class.[40]

This Althusserian conception of the relationship between the base and the superstructure, especially the state and the ideological state apparatuses, came to inform Poulantzas's analysis of classes, class struggle, and the state.

The dominant class maintains its rule over the masses by ideological hegemony not only through the state apparatus, but by other means as well. A critical weapon in the arsenal of capital and the capitalist state in this respect is the ideology of nationalism. Nationalism and nationalist ideology promoted by the capitalist state thus come to serve, and reinforce, the ideological hegemony of the bourgeoisie. In this way, bourgeois nationalism becomes an ideological tool of the capitalist class to protect and advance its class interests, while at the same time diverting the struggles of the working class away from the fight against capitalism and the capitalist state.

Through the use of nationalism and nationalist ideology, the dominant capitalist class has been able to deceive the laboring masses that their problems are caused by other nations and ethnic groups, and not by the capitalists of their own nation. Through such deception, the exploiting class has maintained its moral and cultural sway over the masses to serve its own narrow class interests under the veil of nationalism.

"People always have been the foolish victims of deception and self-deception in politics," Lenin tells us, "and they always will be until they have learnt to seek out the interests of some class or other behind all moral, religious, political and social phrases, declarations and promises."[41] And this is true with the use of nationalism and nationalist ideology as an effective weapon of control and domination in the hands of the bourgeoisie.

Nationalism has served this function for the capitalist class and the capitalist state ever since the formation of nation-states in the eighteenth century. In the period that followed right up to the present, the bourgeoisies of many states have actively promoted nationalism to advance their interests and do so under the cloak of advancing the national interest.

Nationalism, promoted in this manner, thus made its way into the psyche of the broad masses of the population affected by the ideological hegemony exercised by the bourgeoisie to mobilize the nation behind "national" interests that, in essence, only benefited the bourgeoisie. The transformation of bourgeois ideology into a national one to maintain the rule of the capitalist class over the state and society thus accomplished the merger of the two to effectively control mass consciousness so that it developed along national, rather than class, lines. National consciousness, while created and promoted by the national bourgeoisie, thus became embraced by broad segments of the working class and the masses in general, facilitating in this way the class interests of the capitalists while blocking the development of class consciousness that would lead to revolution and topple the rule of capital and the capitalist state.

In examining the class nature of nationalism, and of the state itself, it thus becomes imperative to ask the decisive question: which class controls and dominates the state? An understanding of the class nature of the state (i.e., the centrality of the state as an instrument of class rule) is, therefore, crucial for an understanding of the class nature of nationalism and ethnonational conflict. The forces that promote such conflict by fanning the flames of nationalism are the very same forces that we have come to identify as those that exercise both material and ideological hegemony—and these forces are organized and led by none other than the dominant national bourgeoisie. Bourgeois nationalism is thus the ideological expression of the dominant bourgeois class that has come to impose its rule and the rule of the bourgeois state over society, a topic that will be taken up again in the next chapter.

NOTES

1. G. Glezerman, *Classes and Nations* (Moscow: Progress Publishers, 1979), p. 10.
2. Glezerman, *Classes and Nations*, p. 23.
3. Glezerman, *Classes and Nations*, p. 22.
4. Glezerman, *Classes and Nations*, p. 23.
5. Glezerman, *Classes and Nations*, p. 28.
6. K. Marx quoted in Ralph Dahrendorf, *Class and Class Conflict in Industrial Society* (Stanford, Calif.: Stanford University Press, 1959), p. 18.
7. Marx quoted in Dahrendorf, *Class and Class Conflict in Industrial Society*.
8. Glezerman, *Classes and Nations*, p. 27.
9. Glezerman, *Classes and Nations*, p. 34.
10. Glezerman, *Classes and Nations*, pp. 34–35.
11. Glezerman, *Classes and Nations*, p. 35.

12. Marx quoted in Dahrendorf, *Class and Class Conflict in Industrial Society*, p. 18.

13. M. Adler, "The Ideology of the World War," in *Austro-Marxism*, ed. Tom Bottomore and Patrick Goode (Oxford, U.K.: Oxford University Press, 1978), p. 127.

14. Adler, "The Ideology of the World War," p. 127.

15. Frederick Engels, "The Origin of the Family, Private Property, and the State," in K. Marx and F. Engels, *Selected Works* (New York: International Publishers, 1972), p. 537.

16. Engels, "The Origin of the Family, Private Property, and the State," pp. 587–88.

17. Karl Marx and Frederick Engels, "Manifesto of the Communist Party," in Marx and Engels, *Selected Works*, p. 53.

18. V. I. Lenin, "The State," in K. Marx, F. Engels, and V. I. Lenin, *On Historical Materialism* (New York: International Publishers, 1974), p. 641.

19. Frederick Engels, "Ludwig Feuerbach and the End of Classical German Philosophy," in Marx and Engels, *Selected Works*, p. 627.

20. Marx and Engels, "Manifesto of the Communist Party," p. 37.

21. Goran Therborn, *What Does the Ruling Class Do When It Rules?* (London: New Left Books, 1978), p. 35.

22. Therborn, *What Does the Ruling Class Do When It Rules?* p. 132.

23. Therborn, *What Does the Ruling Class Do When It Rules?* p. 162.

24. Therborn, *What Does the Ruling Class Do When It Rules?* p. 165.

25. Therborn, *What Does the Ruling Class Do When It Rules?* p. 165.

26. Therborn, *What Does the Ruling Class Do When It Rules?* p. 169.

27. Goran Therborn, *Science, Class and Society* (London: New Left Books, 1976), pp. 400–1.

28. Therborn, *What Does the Ruling Class Do When It Rules?* p. 181.

29. Therborn, *What Does the Ruling Class Do When It Rules?* p. 181.

30. Albert Szymanski, *The Capitalist State and the Politics of Class* (Cambridge, Mass.: Winthrop Publishers, 1978), p. 21, 25.

31. Szymanski, *The Capitalist State and the Politics of Class*, p. 24.

32. Szymanski, *The Capitalist State and the Politics of Class*, p.24.

33. Engels, "Ludwig Feuerbach and the End of Classical German Philosophy," p. 627.

34. For a detailed discussion of the political implications of the globalization of capital on the capitalist state and its role in the world economy, see Berch Berberoglu (ed.), *Globalization of Capital and the Nation-State: Imperialism, Class Struggle, and the State in the Age of Global Capitalism* (Lanham, Md.: Rowman & Littlefield, 2003).

35. Berch Berberoglu (ed.), *Labor and Capital in the Age of Globalization: The Labor Process and the Changing Nature of Work in the Global Economy* (Lanham, Md.: Rowman & Littlefield, 2002).

36. Antonio Gramsci, *Prison Notebooks* (New York: International Publishers, 1971), p. 244.

37. See Louis Althusser, *For Marx* (London: Penguin, 1969) and Louis Althusser, *Lenin and Philosophy and Other Essays* (New York: Monthly Review Press, 1971). See also Louis Althusser and Etienne Balibar, *Reading Capital* (London: New Left Books, 1970).

38. Althusser, *Lenin and Philosophy and Other Essays*, p. 185.

39. Nicos Poulantzas, *Political Power and Social Classes* (London: New Left Books, 1974), p. 209.

40. Poulantzas, *Political Power and Social Classes*.

41. V. I. Lenin, "The Three Sources and Three Component Parts of Marxism," in Lenin, *Selected Works in One Volume* (New York: International Publishers, 1971), p. 24.

Chapter Seven

Nationalism, Ethnic Conflict, and Class Struggle

The resurgence of nationalism and ethnic conflict during the past decade marks a turning point in the evolution of the late twentieth- and early twenty-first-century global political economy ushered in by the collapse of the Soviet Union and its allied Eastern European states at century's end. The rise of national movements and ethnonational conflict in a number of regions across the world in recent years highlights the importance of the national question, which continues to persist in the age of globalization. The decisive issue that needs to be taken up for analysis at this critical juncture, however, is the class character and dynamics of these movements as a reflection of underlying class relations.

This chapter examines the broader theoretical and political issues related to the recent resurgence of national movements, nationalist ideology, and ethnonational conflict that has led to civil war and national upheavals. Providing an analysis of the class forces leading such conflict—forces that stand to gain both politically and economically—I argue that the national uprisings and ethnic strife that emanate from these developments are best understood when placed in class perspective, so that one can sort out the relationship between nationalism, ethnic conflict, and class struggle, which have coalesced to bring about the recent epochal social transformations.

NATIONALISM: THE IDEOLOGY OF A RISING BOURGEOISIE

Just as the rising bourgeoisie of the late eighteenth and early nineteenth centuries used nationalism as its battle cry against feudalism in consolidating its power over society, nationalism today is a mobilizing force of the rising national and petty bourgeoisies striving to take state power, most vigorously in the former Soviet republics, Eastern Europe, and in various parts of the capitalist world, especially in formerly colonized regions of the Third World.

While nationalism, like other similar ideologies, can be used by any class to advance particular class-based interests under the cloak of "national unity," the class essence of national identity that such ideology fosters is clearly bound-up with the territory associated with the property-linked interests of a dominant class that is nationally based. Hence, the nationalism of the rising local bourgeoisie is an outcome not of its supposed patriotic allegiance to an imagined national community, but of its nationally based means of production, which it utilizes to exploit wage labor in the local capital accumulation process.

During the development of capitalism since the late eighteenth century, the commercial and industrial interests that merged into a single unified class forming the rising bourgeoisie increasingly viewed their interests as tied up with the nation in which they amassed their growing wealth and came to require the protection of the state to safeguard their increasingly privileged position in society. This led to the control of state power during the transition from feudalism to capitalism in order to advance the interests of capital as distinct from the interests of the overthrown landed aristocracy on the one hand and the emerging working class on the other. The early capitalists thus came to articulate, through the instrumentality of the state, not only their own particular class interests, but appeared to represent the interests of the nation as a whole, hence promoting the illusion that the state is the expression of the national will and that its role is to protect and advance the rights of all citizens.

"At first glance, it may seem that the exploiter state really does express the interests of society as a whole, uniting all of its members within a structure," writes G. Belov:

> But no state has ever existed which served the interests of the exploiters and the exploited in equal measure. In those countries where the minority gathers to itself the bulk of the national wealth, the state primarily acts out as an oppressor of the majority rather than as the promoter of the interests of all citizens. This is the basic postulate one must bear in mind in order to fathom the essence, or the class nature of the state; only then can the true meaning of the state's activities be understood.[1]

"Bourgeois parties," Belov continues, "create the illusion that the bourgeois state expresses the interests of the entire nation."[2] In fact, however, the state in capitalist society expresses the will of the capitalist class to advance the interests of capital at the expense of the working class and other sectors of society and the nation as a whole. To hide this fact, the state uses nationalist ideology to *appear* as the voice of the whole people, while promoting policies that benefit the capitalists alone. In this sense, the nationalist ideology propagated by the state quickly becomes evident as an ideology of the bourgeoisie.

Bourgeois nationalism articulated by the capitalist state thus becomes a weapon in the hands of the capitalists to divide the working class and neutralize its efforts to unite across national boundaries to wage battle against capital and the capitalist state. Nationalist ideology serves to set workers of one nation against those of another to advance the interests of the bourgeoisie and the bourgeois state in various countries in the global rivalry between competing capitalist forces vying for power to control and dominate the world political economy.

While the relationship between capital, the state, and the nation has been a mutually supportive one in the development of capitalism over the past two centuries, nationalism as an ideology of the rising bourgeoisie applies equally to both the classic origins of the bourgeois nation and the newly rising bourgeoisie in the less-developed nations that are in the early stages of capitalist development where the state plays a key role in promoting the expanded accumulation of capital.

The absence or limited presence of the national bourgeoisie in many Third World countries where colonialism and imperialism have historically played a decisive role in blocking the development of an independent national industrial bourgeoisie has led the state to play a more direct role in promoting capitalism and the future development of a strong national capitalist class that would be capable of competing with its counterparts in the global market. The cultivation of such a class through the institutional mechanisms of the state apparatus that involves bourgeois and petty bourgeois elements that are in control of the state has coincided well with the state's promotion of nationalism that would establish a national framework for the future development and expansion of national capitalism in these countries. Hence, the strong hand of the state in both fostering the development of a national bourgeoisie and its use of nationalist ideology to reinforce this role has brought the state to the forefront of its relationship to national bourgeois interests and revealed the essence of nationalism as an ideology of the national bourgeoisie. The fact that this is done largely by the state in the absence of a strong national capitalist class does not alter the nature and role of nationalism as an ideology that promotes the interests of a particular class—the national bourgeoisie.

Nationalism, then, as an ideology of the rising bourgeoisie, is a manifestation of bourgeois class interests expressed through the state beyond the classic temporal and spatial context in which the bourgeois nation-state came into being. Thus, nationalism is a universal ideology of the bourgeoisie, which runs across time, space, and specific national territory. It is an (ideological) extension of the interests of the national bourgeoisie as the dominant class in capitalist society.

ETHNIC CONFLICT:
A PRODUCT OF BOURGEOIS NATIONALISM

The resurgence of nationalism and ethnic conflict during the last decade of the twentieth century, prompted by the collapse of the Soviet Union and its allied East European states, most notably the civil war in the former Yugoslavia, has brought the phenomenon of nationalism and ethnonational conflict to the forefront of intellectual discourse and debate.

The renewed focus on ethnic relations, emerging from the study of ethnonational conflict that has come to define the parameters of social life in societies torn by ethnic strife, has introduced to the discourse on nationalism elements of a bourgeois idealist view that highlights ethnicity as the primary determinant of social conflict. Such emphasis on ethnocultural phenomena has contributed to a distorted view of social reality, where the class basis of ethnonational conflicts that define the nature of nationalism as an ideology of the bourgeoisie is ignored or dismissed in line with the conventional view of the nation and nationalism that I discussed earlier.

"It is obvious," writes G. Glezerman in his book *Classes and Nations*, "that a nation has definite ethnic elements, i.e., it consists of people of different nationalities and tribes which in the course of the formation of a nation merge to form a single whole."[3] "But it is not a nation's ethnic community," Glezerman continues, "that determines its social image; it is shaped by its social nature insofar as the formation of a nation always takes place on the basis of a specific mode of production and under the guidance of a definite class."[4]

This is also the case in relations between nations. "The nature of relations between nations," writes Glezerman, "also depends on their social and political structure. In spite of the fact that in international relations a nation can act as a more or less compact whole, these relations depend on the class or classes which are predominant in a nation."[5] The dominant class or classes that control the state thus define a nation's relations with other nations.

Ethnic conflict and ethnonational strife are, in fact, the outcome of dominant class forces in society attempting to advance their class interests, both domestically and on a world scale. Thus, in capitalist society, the classes that foster and in turn benefit from such conflict are the national and petty bourgeoisies whose ideology is bourgeois nationalism.

Bourgeois nationalism appears in many forms in different spatial and temporal settings. "Like any other social phenomenon," some have pointed out, "nationalism is not immutable":

> It alters its forms, its place and role in the life of society. New elements appear in its content. Its links with other social phenomena change. And this poses new questions. In our time, for example, with the danger of nationalism so much greater for the world revolutionary process, special importance attaches to the method of approach to such questions as the relation of the class element to the national element, and of the international to the national, the interrelation of the national and nationalist, and the real historical place, social role, essence and content of the different manifestations of nationalism.[6]

All of these point to the fact that nationalism and ethnic conflict are a manifestation of class interests and class forces that invoke national and ethnic symbolism to advance their own narrow class project and do so in the name of the nation or ethnic group they claim to represent.

While historically the national bourgeoisie has been the leading force in advocating nationalism to advance bourgeois interests, the form and content of nationalism has varied over time when in different contexts forces other than the national bourgeoisie have taken the lead to promote "national" interests. Thus, while "nationalism does not exist in a pure form, is always closely associated with political, juridical, religious and other social views,"[7] it is, nevertheless, based on the dynamics of social class and class struggle that have political implications. Thus, as James Blaut also points out, while there are "many forms and combination of national struggle," each of these struggles "must display a certain pattern of class participation (on both sides of the struggle, needless to say), and hence is subject to class analysis like any other moment of the class struggle—of which national struggle is one type."[8] National struggle, then, Blaut concludes, "is one form or category of the struggle to seize state power."[9] And this has occurred in a variety of settings in which such forces have come to assume political power.

In extreme cases, bourgeois and petty bourgeois nationalism has led to brutal dictatorships, violent ethnocentrism, and xenophobia, with all their ultra-national racist manifestations. Such regimes have incited war and committed genocide in the past, and similar developments today threaten to erupt into conflicts that foster ethnic, racial, and national divisions that may lead to grave social consequences.

Ethnic conflict, arising from national, cultural, racial, and other differences among people that the bourgeois forces have come to promote in their effort to take (or hold on to) state power, is in essence a product of bourgeois and petty bourgeois nationalism. The bourgeois forces have manipulated national feelings and ethnic identity of the masses in various ways in order to advance their own narrow, nationally based property interests. In so doing, they have enlisted the state or developed their own reactionary, ultranationalist organizations to safeguard their interests. In this sense, the multitude of conflicts arising from deep-seated class antagonisms that are endemic to capitalist society have been diverted to ethnic and ethnonational conflicts that serve nationalist ends. Thus, bourgeois nationalism has been in a very real sense the driving force of ethnic conflict fostered by bourgeois forces intent on advancing national capitalist interests. And this they have done through the central role of the capitalist state, which has come to serve as their repressive political arm.

CLASS STRUGGLE: THE DRIVING FORCE OF ETHNONATIONAL CONFLICT

As I have argued throughout this book, a close examination of the nature and dynamics of ethnonational conflict in the world today reveals the class nature of this phenomenon that is driven by the logic of class struggle orchestrated by various nationalist forces in society. Identification of the national and petty bourgeoisies as the leading classes promoting ethnic and national divisions in line with their nationally based class interests has led us to an analysis of the class nature of nationalism and ethnic conflict as part of the process of class struggle within which questions related to the nation and nationalism have emerged.

Class struggle is the driving force of ethnonational conflict and civil war precisely because the clashing interests of various antagonistic classes are played out at the national level under the banner of nationalism. Nationalism and ethnonational conflict are thus manifestations of a deeper struggle for political and economic power that social classes strive for when locked in contradictory class positions that are diametrically opposed, that cannot be resolved in any way except in open conflict that erupts into civil war—a war that is in essence an open struggle between opposing classes vying for state power. An alliance of class forces built upon a broad national appeal to win over the masses to the side of a winning strategy is what makes the difference in success or failure of a national movement that is class based and is driven by the dynamics of class forces engaged in a class struggle.

Notwithstanding the universal appeal of nationalist ideology catering to the cultural, religious, and national aspirations of broad segments of the population longing for freedom, dignity, and social and personal identity, nationalism and ethnonationalist ideology promoted by dominant (or rival) classes serve to mobilize mass discontent to advance the interests of particular dominant (or ascendant) class forces that are engaged in struggle for power—a struggle that *appears* to be national in scope but is in fact driven by its *class* dynamics.

The class nature of nationalism and ethnic conflict is clearly evident when one examines the class basis of national movements that are waging battle to take (or to sustain) state power. While such movements may be based on an alliance of social forces driven by a multitude of class and group interests, the fundamental *class* character of the leading elements within such forces becomes evident as soon as the parameters of the national struggle are defined and the boundaries of the struggle for power are revealed. It is in this context of the struggle for power that the national movement (and the ethnonational conflicts it engenders) comes to show its real, *class* character and *class* content hidden under the veil of nation and nationalist ideology.

The essence of prevailing resurgent forms of nationalism and ethnic conflict that engulf the world today is thus to be found in the underlying class configurations of society made up of antagonistic class forces that are engaged in a life-and-death struggle to exert or to maintain their dominance over society—a struggle that is clearly class based, and national in appearance only.

Nationalism and ethnic conflict, therefore, are manifestations of class conflict and class struggle and originate from the class structure and class composition of society that is divided along class lines. It is, in the end, these very class forces that exert themselves and use nationalism, much like religion and other ideologies, as a mobilizing force to achieve political power and control over society.

The diverse settings in which nationalist movements have emerged and developed necessitate a careful analysis of the dynamics of this process, which is central to our understanding of class, state, nation, and ethnicity—phenomena that are in turn critical to our understanding of the nature and dynamics of nationalism, class struggle, and social transformation. It is thus within the framework of an understanding of the relationship between these phenomena that we find the social relevance of nationalism and national movements as manifested in different spatial, temporal, and political contexts. An analysis of the class nature of national movements, then, provides us a clear understanding of the nature, form, and class content of nationalism, as well as the nature and dynamics of the society that a given movement is attempting to build. With a clear class perspective on the ideology of nationalism and national movements, we can thus better understand this powerful and persistent phenomenon that has once again gripped the attention of the world community in the late twentieth and early twenty-first centuries.

Nationalism, ethnic conflict, and class struggle are part and parcel of the process of national development led by the national bourgeoisie under conditions of developing and mature capitalism, historically and today. They are the end result of a protracted political struggle that has brought to power bourgeois and petty bourgeois forces and their class allies who will benefit from such conflict. But the very dynamic that brought the bourgeois forces to power is now threatening the very basis of the established social order, as working people across the globe are beginning to exercise their collective will through organized political action—a response that is in the making and will become more and more apparent in the current century.

NOTES

1. G. Belov, *What Is the State?* (Moscow: Progress Publishers, 1986), pp. 22–23.

2. Belov, *What Is the State?* p. 23.

3. G. Glezerman, *Classes and Nations* (Moscow: Progress Publishers, 1979), p. 24.

4. Glezerman, *Classes and Nations*, p. 24.

5. Glezerman, *Classes and Nations*, p. 25.

6. V. Zagladin, ed., *The Revolutionary Movement of Our Time and Nationalism* (Moscow: Progress Publishers, 1975), p. 25.

7. Zagladin, *The Revolutionary Movement of Our Time and Nationalism*, p. 25.

8. James M. Blaut, *The National Question: Decolonizing the Theory of Nationalism* (London: Zed Books, 1987), p. 123.

9. Blaut, *The National Question*, p. 123.

Conclusion

Class, state, and nation are the driving forces of nationalism and ethnic conflict that have come to define the nature of social relations that are at base a manifestation of class struggles in society. I have attempted to show the class nature of nationalism and ethnonational conflict, both theoretically and empirically, through an analysis of nationalism as an ideology stemming from and serving the interests of a particular class or an alliance of classes, and by providing a series of case studies of nationalism and ethnonational conflict in advanced capitalist, Third World, and socialist settings during the course of the twentieth century.

I have argued that nations are real (not imagined) communities and exist as collective units with definite cultural, linguistic, territorial, and social characteristics. Moreover, these unique attributes are a manifestation of specific historical and social processes that are based on class relations and class struggles. While a number of classes make up the totality of a nation, only one class (or an alliance of several classes led by one class) dominates the economic, political, and social life of society and determines its course of development. Hence, nationalism, as an ideology of a particular class—that is, the bourgeoisie—serves as the dominant ideology in a nation ruled by that class. The state in this type of society, therefore, comes to reflect the interests of the dominant, ruling class (the bourgeoisie), hence it is characterized as the bourgeois state.

Analysis of the relationship between state and nation has also revealed the fact that while the state presides over the nation as the sole representative of the national will, it does so by playing a decisive role that is class driven. Hence, the representation the state provides for the nation, I argue, is indeed a narrow one—one that reflects the interests of the dominant ruling class that controls the state. The nation, therefore, is not a collective expression of an entire people represented by the state; it is, instead, the expression of the interests of a particular *class* under nationalist ideological cover that conceals the class nature of the state and the class essence of the nation and nationalism that the state so skillfully articulates. It is for this reason that I have placed much emphasis on the class nature of the state and nation, as well as of the ideology of nationalism.

An examination of the relationship between class and nation, class and state, and state and nation inevitably raises questions on the triangular relationship between class, state, and nation, which, as I have argued, together constitute the pillars of nationalism and ethnic conflict in contemporary capitalist society. Driven by the logic of capitalism and capitalist relations, the modern nation-state has evolved to become the chief political agent of capital and the capitalist class under conditions of developing and mature capitalism. The class struggle and the revolutionary process that emerge out of these relationships are reflections of social conditions in society based on antagonistic class relations that are historically determined. Nationalism, as the ideology of the national bourgeoisie, thus emerges from this process as a reflection of the interests of the capitalist class that has come to control the modern nation-state.

In the Third World, while nationalism and national movements have followed a similar logic as that in the advanced capitalist countries, the anticolonial and anti-imperialist national liberation struggles have sometimes been won by a coalition of class forces led by the working class and the peasantry, and at other times by a populist coalition led by the petty bourgeoisie. The mobilization of the masses by a national movement under the leadership of petty bourgeois forces on one hand, and under working class leadership on the other, have come to represent two competing strands in Third-World nationalist movements that are quite different from their bourgeois counterparts in the advanced capitalist countries.

While nationalism is, by definition, the ideology of the national bourgeoisie, the critical factor that distinguishes bourgeois nationalism from other forms of nationalism utilized by progressive forces to mobilize the masses in a national liberation struggle is the *class nature* of the national movement and its leadership—a condition that determines the nature and parameters of the national struggle and sets the limits to the course of development that may or may not challenge the prevailing class structure and class relations.

Whereas a national movement directed against imperialism led by the national and petty bourgeoisies may have an antifeudal and pro-capitalist outcome (as in Egypt in the 1950s and 1960s), a similar anti-imperialist national struggle led by the working class allied with the peasantry and other popular segments of society may wage an antifeudal *and* anticapitalist campaign and fight for socialism (as has been the case historically in China and Cuba).

The use of nationalist ideology by working-class organizations to mobilize the masses, responding to their yearning for national identity and independence under colonial and neocolonial conditions, is something entirely different than the nationalist call by the bourgeois forces that use nationalism as an extension of their narrow, nationally based class interests, portraying it as the general national interest.

The analysis developed in this book regarding the class nature of nationalism and ethnic conflict plays a central role in situating the state in this process. The state, as the chief superstructural institution in society, acquires the authority to represent the interests of the dominant class and regulates the class struggle in favor of capital and the capitalist class, while at the same time rendering a modicum of benefits to wage labor and other sectors of society and allowing certain basic individual and collective rights. Thus, in this sense, the nationalist ideology propagated by the state is an expression of the interests of the class that controls the state, while the state is mandated to cover up this fact and to give it broad societal expression that nationalism and national identity come to represent. In instances when nationalist ideology is used by political organizations of the working class and other laboring sections of society to assure a popular victory, the victorious state comes to represent the interests of the laboring masses and embarks on a popular, working-class project that is in line with the interests of the class or classes that now control the state. Hence, in this sense, one can speak of the establishment of a socialist state.

Following on our analysis of the class nature of the state, nation, nationalism, and ethnic conflict, it is hoped that future studies of the nation and nationalism will begin to pay closer attention to the nature and dynamics of the class forces that are behind ideological phenomena and examine them in class terms. For only through a class analysis of social forces and their ideological manifestations will we be able to clearly understand (and change) the nature and course of development of society and social relations—a process strongly affected by the phenomenon of nationalism.

Bibliography

Abdel-Malek, Anouar. 1981. *Nation and Revolution*. Albany: State University of New York Press.

Abdelal, Rawi. 2001. *National Purpose in the World Economy: Post-Soviet States in Comparative Perspective*. Ithaca, N.Y.: Cornell University Press.

Abdo, Nahla. 1991. "Women of the Intifada: Gender, Class and National Liberation," *Race and Class* 32, no. 4.

Abed-Rabbo, Samir, and D. Safie. 1990. *The Palestinian Uprising*. Belmont, Mass.: Association of Arab-American University Graduates.

Acuna, Rodolfo. 1988. *Occupied America*. 3rd ed. New York: Harper & Row.

Adam, Jan. 2000. *The Social Costs of Transformation in Post-Socialist Countries: The Cases of Poland, the Czech Republic and Hungary*. New York: Palgrave.

Alder, M. 1978. "The Ideology of the World War." *Austro-Marxism*, ed. Tom Bottomore and Patrick Goode. Oxford, U.K.: Oxford Univerity Press.

Ahmida, Ali Abdullatif, ed. 2000. *Beyond Colonialism and Nationalism in the Maghrib: History, Culture, and Politics*. Hampshire, U.K.: Palgrave Macmillan.

Alter, Peter. 1989. *Nationalism*. London: Edward Arnold.

Amin, Samir. 1980. *Class and Nation, Historically and in the Current Crisis*. New York: Monthly Review Press.

Anderson, Benedict. 1983. *Imagined Communities: Reflections on the Origin and Spread of Nationalism*. London: Verso.

Anderson, Malcolm. 2000. *States and Nationalism in Europe since 1945*. New York: Routledge.

Andor, Laszlo, and Martin Summers. 1998. *Market Failure: A Guide to the East European "Economic Miracle."* London: Pluto Press.

Armstrong, J. 1982. *Nations Before Nationalism*. Chapel Hill: University of North Carolina Press.

Arrighi, Giovanni, and John S. Saul. 1969. "Nationalism and Revolution in Sub-Saharan Africa," *The Socialist Register*. London: Merlin.

Aruri, Naseer. 1970. *The Palestine Resistance to Israeli Occupation*. Wilmette, Ill.: Medina University Press International.

———, ed. 1983. *Occupation: Israel over Palestine*. Belmont, Mass.: Association of Arab-American University Graduates.

Ashraf, A. 1983. "Bazaar and Mosque in Iran's Revolution." *MERIP Reports* 13, no. 3 (March–April).

Aughey, Arthur. 2001. *Nationalism, Devolution and the Challenge to the United Kingdom State*. London: Pluto Press.

Bairner, Alan. 2001. *Sport, Nationalism, and Globalization: European and North American Perspectives*. Albany: State University of New York Press.

Bakhash, S. 1983. *The Reign of the Ayatollahs*. New York: Basic.

Balibar, Etienne, and Immanuel Wallerstein. 1991. *Race, Nation, Class*. London: Verso.

Balkan, Nesecan, and Sungur Savran, eds. 2002. *The Politics of Permanent Crisis: Class, Ideology, and State in Turkey*. New York: Nova Science Publishers.

Bannerji, Himani, et al., eds. 2001. *Of Property and Propriety: The Role of Gender and Class in Imperialism and Nationalism*. Toronto: University of Toronto Press.

Barlow, Andrew L. 2003. *Between Fear and Hope: Globalization and Race in the United States*. Lanham, Md.: Rowman & Littlefield.

Barreto, Amilcar A. 1998. *Language, Elites and the State: Nationalism in Puerto Rico and Quebec*. Westport, Conn.: Praeger.

Barzani, Masud, and Ahmed Ferhadi, eds. 2003. *Mustafa Barzani and the Kurdish Liberation Movement*. London: Palgrave Macmillan.

Bauer, Otto, and Ephraim J. Nimni, eds. 2000. *The Question of Nationalities and Social Democracy*. Minneapolis: University of Minnesota Press.

Baum, Gregory. 2001. *Nationalism, Religion, and Ethics*. Toronto: McGill-Queens University Press.

Beiner, Ronald, ed. 1999. *Theorizing Nationalism*. Albany: State University of New York Press.

Beissinger, Mark R. 2002. *Nationalist Mobilization and the Collapse of the Soviet State*. Cambridge, U.K.: Cambridge University Press.

Belov, G. 1986. *What Is the State?* Moscow: Progress Publishers.

Ben-Ami, Shlomo, Yoav Peled, and Alberto Spektorowski, eds. 2000. *Ethnic Challenges to the Modern Nation State*. New York: Palgrave.

Berberoglu, Berch. 1982. *Turkey in Crisis: From State Capitalism to Neocolonialism*. London: Zed Books.

———. 1987. *The Internationalization of Capital: Imperialism and Capitalist Development on a World Scale*. New York: Praeger.

———. 1991. "Nationalism and Ethnic Rivalry in the Early Twentieth Century," *Nature, Society, and Thought* 4, no. 3.

———. 1992. *The Political Economy of Development: Development Theory and the Prospects for Change in the Third World*. Albany: State University of New York Press.

———. 1994. *Class Structure and Social Transformation*. New York: Praeger.

———. 1999. *Turmoil in the Middle East: Imperialism, War, and Political Instability*. Albany: State University of New York Press.

———. 2001. *Political Sociology: A Comparative/Historical Approach*. 2nd ed. New York: General Hall.

———. 2003. *The Globalization of Capital and the Nation-State*. Lanham, Md.: Rowman & Littlefield.

———, ed. 1989. *Power and Stability in the Middle East*. London: Zed Books.

———. 1992. *Class, State, and Development in India*. New Delhi: Sage.

———. 1995. *The National Question: Nationalism, Ethnic Conflict, and Self-Determination in the Twentieth Century*. Philadelphia: Temple University Press.

———. 2002. *Labor and Capital in the Age of Globalization*. Lanham, Md.: Rowman & Littlefield.

Besikci, Ismail. 1988. *Kurdistan: An Interstate Colony*. Sydney: Australian Kurdish Association.

———. 1991. *The State of Terror in the Middle East*. Ankara, Turkey: Yurt Kitap Yayinlari.

Bhana, Surendra. 1975. *The United States and the Development of the Puerto Rican Status Question 1936–1968*. Wichita: The University Press of Kansas.

Birch, Anthony H. 1989. *Nationalism and National Integration*. London: Unwin Hyman.

Blaut, James M. 1987. *The National Question: Decolonizing the Theory of Nationalism*. London: Zed Books.

Blom, Ida, et al., ed. 2000. *Gendered Nations: Nationalisms and Gender Order in the Nineteenth Century*. New York: New York University Press.

Bluckert, Kjell, and John St. H. Gibaut. 2000. *The Church as Nation: A Study in Ecclesiology and Nationhood*. New York: Peter Lang Publishing.

Bourque, Gilles. 1977. *L'Etat Capitaliste et la Question Nationale*. Montréal: Presses de l'Université de Montréal.

———. 1984. "Class, Nation, and the Parti Québécois." In *Quebec, State and Society*, ed. Alain G. Gagnon. Toronto: Methuen.

———. 1995. "Quebec Nationalism and the Struggle for Sovereignty in French Canada." In *The National Question: Nationalism, Ethnic Conflict and Self-Determination in the Twentieth Century*, ed. Berch Berberoglu. Philadelphia: Temple University Press.

Boyle, Francis A. 2003. *Palestine, Palestinians and International Law*. Atlanta: Clarity Press.

Brehony, Kevin J., and Naz Rassool, eds. 1999. *Nationalisms Old and New*. Hampshire, U.K.: Palgrave Macmillan.

Breuilly, John. 1994. *Nationalism and the State*. 2nd ed. Chicago: University of Chicago Press.

Brown, David. 2000. *Contemporary Nationalism: Civic, Ethnocultural, and Multicultural Politics*. New York: Routledge.

Brown, Michael E., ed. 1993. *Ethnic Conflict and International Security*. Princeton, N.J.: Princeton University Press.

Brown, Michael E., et al., eds. 2001. *Nationalism and Ethnic Conflict*. Rev. ed. Cambridge, Mass.: MIT Press.

Brubaker, Rogers. 1992. *Citizenship and Nationhood in France and Germany*. Cambridge, Mass.: Harvard Univerity Press.

———. 1996. *Nationalism Reframed: Nationhood and the National Question in the New Europe*. Cambridge, U.K.: Cambridge University Press.

Brudny, Yitzhak M. 1999. *Reinventing Russia: Russian Nationalism and the Soviet State, 1953–1991*. Cambridge, Mass.: Harvard University Press.

Bruinessen, Martin Van. 1984. "The Kurds in Turkey." *Middle East Report* 121.

———. 1992. *Agha, Shaikh, and State: The Social and Political Structures of Kurdistan*. London: Zed Books.

Calhoun, Craig. 1997. *Nationalism*. Minneapolis: University of Minnesota Press.

Canovan, Margaret. 1996. *Nationhood and Political Theory*. Chelthenham, U.K.: Edward Elgar.

Caplan, Richard, and John Feffer, eds. 1996. *Europe's New Nationalism*. New York: Oxford University Press.

Carey, Roane, ed. 2001. *The New Intifada: Resisting Israel's Apartheid*. London: Verso.

Carmichael, Cathie. 2002. *Ethnic Cleansing in the Balkans: Nationalism and the Destruction of Tradition*. New York: Routledge.

Carr, Robert. 2002. *Black Nationalism in the New World: Reading the African American and West Indian Experience*. Durham, N.C.: Duke University Press.

Chafetz, Glenn R., et al., eds. 1999. *Origins of National Interests*. Portland, Ore.: Frank Cass.

Chaliand, Gerard. 1972. *The Palestinian Resistance*. Baltimore, Md.: Penguin.

———. 1980. *People without a Country: The Kurds and Kurdistan*. London: Zed Books.

———. 1994. *The Kurdish Tragedy*. London: Zed Books.

Chandler, David. 2000. *Bosnia: Faking Democracy after Dayton*. London: Pluto Press.

Chandra, Bipan. 1975. "The Indian Capitalist Class and Imperialism before 1947," *Journal of Contemporary Asia* 5, no. 3.

Chatterji, Rakhahari. 2001. *Working Class and the Nationalist Movement in India: The Critical Years*. International Academic Publishers.

Chennells, David. 2001. *The Politics of Nationalism in Canada: Cultural Conflict since 1760*. Toronto: University of Toronto Press.

Chirot, Daniel, and Martin E. P. Seligman, eds. 2001. *Ethnopolitical Warfare: Causes, Consequences, and Possible Solutions*. Washington, D.C.: American Psychological Association.

Choueiri, Youssef M. 2000. *Arab Nationalism—A History: Nation and State in the Arab World*. Oxford, U.K.: Blackwell Publishers.

———. 2001. *Arab Nationalism: A History: Nation and State in the Arab World*. Malden, Mass.: Blackwell Publishers.

Chulos, Chris J., and Timo Piirainen, eds. 2000. *The Fall of an Empire, the Birth of a Nation: National Identities in Russia*. Sudbury, Mass.: Dartmouth.

Churchill, Ward. 1997. *A Little Matter of Genocide: Holocaust and Denial in the Americas, 1492 to the Present*. San Francisco, Calif.: City Lights Books.

Clark, Robert. 1979. *The Basques: The Franco Years and Beyond*. Reno: University of Nevada Press.

———. 1984. *The Basque Insurgents: ETA 1952–1980.* Madison: University of Wisconsin Press.

Clarke, Desmond M., and Charles Jones, eds. 1999. *The Rights of Nations: Nations and Nationalism in a Changing World.* New York: St. Martin's.

Cobban, Alfred. 1970. *The Nation State and National Self-Determination.* New York: Thomas Y. Crowell.

Cobban, Helena. 1984. *The Palestinian Liberation Organization.* Cambridge, U.K.: Cambridge University Press.

Cocks, Joan. 2002. *Passion and Paradox: Intellectuals Confront the National Question.* Princeton, N.J.: Princeton University Press.

Connor, Walker. 1994. *Ethnonationalism: The Quest for Understanding.* Princeton, N.J.: Princeton University Press.

Conversi, Daniele. 2002. *Ethnonationalism in the Contemporary World: Walker Connor and the Study of Nationalism.* New York: Routledge.

———, ed. 2002. *Ethnonationalism in the Contemporary World: Walker Connor and the Study of Nationalism.* London: Routledge.

Cooley, John. 1973. *Green March, Black September.* London: Frank Cass.

Corcuera, Javier, et al. 2002. *The Origins of Basque Nationalism.* Reno: University of Nevada Press.

Cottam, Martha L., and Richard W. Cottam. 2001. *Nationalism & Politics: The Political Behavior of Nation States.* Boulder, Colo.: Rienner.

Croucher, Sheila L. 2004. *Globalization and Belonging: The Politics of Identity in a Changing World.* Lanham, Md.: Rowman & Littlefield.

Dadrian, Vahakn N. 1995. *The History of the Armenian Genocide: Ethnic Conflict from the Balkans to Anatolia to the Caucasus.* Providence, R.I.: Berghahn.

Dahbour, Omar. 1999. *The Nationalism Reader.* Atlantic Highlands, N.J.: Humanities Press International, Inc.

———. 2003. *Illusion of the Peoples: A Critique of National Self-Determination.* Lanham, Md.: Lexington.

Dahrendorf, Ralf. 1959. *Class and Class Conflict in Industrial Society.* Stanford, Calif.: Stanford University Press.

Dallmayr, Fred, and Jose M. Rosales, eds. 2001. *Beyond Nationalism?* Lanham, Md.: Lexington.

Danspeckgruber, Wolfgang, ed. 2002. *The Self-Determination of Peoples: Community, Nation, and State in an Interdependent World.* Boulder, Colo.: Rienner.

Davidson, Basil. 1961. *The African Slave Trade.* Boston: Little, Brown.

Davidson, Neil. 2000. *The Origins of Scottish Nationhood.* London: Pluto Press.

Davis, Horace B. 1967. *Nationalism and Socialism: Marxist and Labor Theories of Nationalism to 1917.* New York: Monthly Review Press.

———. 1978. *Toward a Marxist Theory of Nationalism.* New York: Monthly Review Press.

Dawahare, Anthony. 2002. *Nationalism, Marxism, and African American Literature between the Wars: A New Pandora's Box.* Jackson: University Press of Mississippi.

Debray, Régis. 1967. *Revolution in the Revolution?* New York: Monthly Review Press.

———. 1977. "Marxism and the National Question: Interview with Regis Debray." *New Left Review* 105.

Del Giudice, Luisa, and Gerald Porter, eds. 2001. *Imagined States: Nationalism, Utopia, and Longing in Oral Cultures.* Logan: Utah State University Press.

Denitch, Bogdan. 1994. *Ethnic Nationalism: The Tragic Death of Yugoslavia.* Minneapolis: University of Minnesota Press.

Deol, Harnick. 2000. *Religion and Nationalism in India: The Case of the Punjab.* New York: Routledge.

Deutsch, Karl. 1953. *Nationalism and Social Communication.* Cambridge, Mass.: MIT Press.

Dietz, James L. 1986. *Economic History of Puerto Rico: Institutional Changes and Capitalist Development.* Princeton, N.J.: Princeton University Press.

Dimitrov, Georgi. 1974. *The United Front against Fascism.* New York: Gamma.

Dixon, R., ed. 1972. *Ireland and the Irish Question.* New York: International Publishers.

Donini, Antonio, Norah Niland, and Karin Wermester, eds. 2004. *Nation-Building Unraveled?: Aid, Peace, and Justice in Afghanistan.* Bloomfield, Conn.: Kumarian Press.

Douglass, William A., Carmelo Urza, Linda White, and Joseba Zulaika, eds. 2000. *Basque Politics and Nationalism on the Eve of the Millennium.* Reno: University of Nevada Press.

Doyle, Don Harrison. 2002. *Nations Divided: America, Italy, and the Southern Question.* Athens: University of Georgia Press.

Duncan, Raymond W., and Paul G. Holman Jr., eds. 1994. *Ethnic Nationalism and Regional Conflict.* Boulder, Colo.: Westview.

Dutt, Palme R. 1974. *Fascism and Social Revolution.* San Francisco: Proletarian.

Eley, Geoff, and Ronald Grigor Suny, eds. 1996. *Becoming National.* New York: Oxford University Press.

Engels, Frederick. 1972. "The Origin of the Family, Private Property, and the State." In K. Marx and F. Engels, *Selected Works.* New York: International Publishers.

Eriksen, Thomas Hylland. 2002. *Ethnicity and Nationalism: Anthropological Perspectives.* 2nd ed. London: Pluto Press.

Falola, Toyin. 2001. *Nationalism and African Intellectuals.* Rochester, N.Y.: University of Rochester Press.

Farhi, Farideh. 1989. "Class Struggles, the State, and Revolution in Iran." In *Power and Stability in the Middle East*, ed. Berch Berberoglu. London: Zed Books.

Farsoun, Samih. 1982. "Israel's Goal of Destroying the PLO Is Not Achievable." *Journal of Palestine Studies* 11, no. 4.

Farsoun, Samih, and Jean M. Landis. 1990. "The Sociology of an Uprising: The Roots of the *Intifada*." In *Intifada: Palestine at the Crossroads*, ed. Jamal R. Nassar and Roger Heacock. New York: Praeger.

Farsoun, Samih, and Christina Zacharia. 1997. *Palestine and the Palestinians.* Boulder, Colo.: Westview.

Fenton, Steve, and Stephen May, eds. 2002. *Ethnonational Identities.* Hampshire, U.K.: Palgrave Macmillan.

Fevre, Ralph, and Andrew Thompson, eds. 2000. *Nation, Identity and Social Theory: Perspectives from Wales.* Cardiff, U.K.: University of Wales Press.

Fine, Robert. 1989. "The Antinomies of Nationalism and Democracy in the South African Liberation Struggle." *Review of African Political Economy* 45/46.

Foran, John. 1993. *Fragile Resistance: Social Transformation in Iran from 1500 to the Revolution.* Boulder, Colo.: Westview.

———, ed. 1994. "The Iranian Revolution of 1977–79: A Challenge for Social Theory." In *A Century of Revolution: Social Movements in Iran,* ed. John Foran. Minneapolis: University of Minnesota Press.

Fournier, P. 1981. *Capitalisme et Politique au Québec.* Montréal: Albert Saint-Martin.

Frangi, Abdallah. 1983. *The PLO and Palestine.* London: Zed Books.

Friedman, Jonathan. 2003. *Globalization, the State, and Violence.* Lanham, Md.: AltaMira Press.

Gaffikin, Frank, and Mike Morrissey. 1990. *Northern Ireland: The Thatcher Years.* London: Zed Books.

Gelber, Harry Gregor. 2001. *Nations Out of Empires: European Nationalism and the Transformation of Asia.* New York: St. Martin's.

Gellner, Ernest. 1983. *Nations and Nationalism.* Ithaca, N.Y.: Cornell University Press.

———. 1994. *Encounters with Nationalism.* Malden, Mass.: Blackwell.

Genet, Jean. 1983. "Four Hours in Shatila." *Journal of Palestine Studies* 12, no. 2.

Ghareeb, Edmund. 1981. *The Kurdish Question in Iraq.* Syracuse, N.Y.: Syracuse University Press.

Ghassemlou, Abdul Rahman. 1965. *Kurdistan and the Kurds.* London: Collets.

Giddens, Anthony. 1981. *A Contemporary Critique of Historical Materialism.* Berkeley: University of California Press.

———. 1985. *The Nation-State and Violence.* Berkeley: University of California Press.

Gilbert, Paul. 1998. *The Philosophy of Nationalism.* Boulder, Colo.: Westview.

Glenny, Misha. 2001. *The Balkans: Nationalism, War and the Great Powers 1809–1999.* New York: Penguin.

Glezerman, G. 1979. *Classes and Nations.* Moscow: Progress Publishers.

Gocek, Fatma Muge, ed. 2002. *Social Constructions of Nationalism in the Middle East.* Albany: State University of New York Press.

Goldenberg, Suzanne. 1994. *Pride of Small Nations: The Caucasus and Post-Soviet Disorder.* London: Zed Books.

Goldmann, Kjell, Ulf Hannerz, and Charles Westin, eds. 2000. *Nationalism and Internationalism in the Post Cold-War Era.* New York: Routledge.

Gordon, Hayim, Rivca Gordon, and Taher Shriteh, eds. 2003. *Beyond Intifada: Narrative of Freedom Fighters in the Gaza Strip.* Westport, Conn.: Praeger.

Gordy, Eric D. 1999. *The Culture of Power in Serbia: Nationalism and the Destruction of Alternatives.* University Park: The Pennsylvania State University Press.

Gott, Richard. 1970. *Guerrilla Movements in Latin America.* London: Thomas Nelson.

Gould, Carol, and Pasquale Paquino, eds. 2001. *Cultural Identity and the Nation-State.* Lanham, Md.: Rowman & Littlefield.

Gramsci, Antonio. 1971. *Prison Notebooks.* New York: International Publishers.

Greenfeld, Liah. 1992. *Nationalism: Five Roads to Modernity*. Cambridge, Mass.: Harvard University Press.

Gresh, Alain. 1985. *The PLO: The Struggle Within*. London: Zed Books.

Guerin, Daniel. 1945. *Fascism and Big Business*. New York: Monad Press.

Guibernau, Montserrat, 1999. *Nations without States: Political Communities in a Global Age*. Malden, Mass.: Blackwell.

Guibernau, Montserrat, and John Hutchinson, eds. 2001. *Understanding Nationalism*. Cambridge, U.K.: Polity Press.

Gunter, Michael M. 1991. *The Kurds in Turkey: A Political Dilemma*. Westport, Conn.: Greenwood.

Gupta, Dipankar. 2001. *Culture, Space and the Nation-State: From Sentiment to Structure*. Thousand Oaks, Calif.: Sage.

Haas, Ernst B., and Peter Katzenstein, eds. 2000. *Nationalism, Liberalism, and Progress, Volume 2: The Dismal Fate of New Nations*. Ithaca, N.Y.: Cornell University Press.

Hagendoorn, Louk, György Csepeli, Henk Dekker, and Russell Farnen, eds. 2000. *European Nations and Nationalism: Theoretical and Historical Perspectives*. Burlington, Vt.: Ashgate.

Hall, John A., ed. 1998. *The State of the Nation: Ernest Gellner and the Theory of Nationalism*. Cambridge, U.K.: Cambridge University Press.

Hall, Patrik. 1998. *The Social Construction of Nationalism: Sweden as an Example*. Lund, Sweden: Lund University Press.

Halliday, Fred. 1979. *Iran: Dictatorship and Development*. New York: Penguin.

———. 2000. *Nation and Religion in the Middle East*. Boulder, Colo.: Rienner.

Halpern, Joel Martin, and David A. Kideckel, eds. 2000. *Neighbors at War: Anthropological Perspectives on Yugoslav Ethnicity, Culture, and History*. University Park: The Pennsylvania State University Press.

Harris, Erika. 2002. *Nationalism and Democratization: Politics of Slovakia and Slovenia*. Burlington, Vt.: Ashgate.

Harris, Nigel. 1990. *National Liberation*. London: I. B. Tauris.

Hastings, Adrian. 1997. *The Construction of Nationhood: Ethnicity, Religion, and Nationalism*. Cambridge, U.K.: Cambridge University Press.

———. 1998. *The Construction of Nationhood: Ethnicity, Religion and Nationalism*. Cambridge, U.K.: Cambridge University Press.

Hayes, Carlton J. H. 1937. *Essays on Nationalism*. New York: Macmillan.

———. 1960. *Nationalism: A Religion*. New York: Macmillan.

He, Baogang, and Yingjie Guo. 2000. *Nationalism, National Identity and Democratization in China*. Burlington, Vt.: Ashgate.

Healey, Joseph F. 1995. *Race, Ethnicity, Gender, and Class*. Thousand Oaks, Calif.: Pine Forge Press.

Hechter, Michael. 2002. *Containing Nationalism*. New York: Oxford University Press.

Heideking, Jürgen, Genevieve Fabre, and Kai Dreisbach, eds. 2001. *Celebrating Ethnicity and Nation: American Festive Culture from the Revolution to the Early Twentieth Century*. New York: Berghahn.

Hiro, Dilip. 1993. *Lebanon: Fire and Embers; a History of the Lebanese Civil War*. New York: St. Martin's.

Hobsbawm, Eric. 1962. *The Age of Revolution: 1789–1848.* New York: World.

———. 1972. "Some Reflections on Nationalism." In *Imagination and Precision in the Social Sciences*, ed. T. Nossiter, et al. London: Faber and Faber.

———. 1975. *The Age of Capital: 1848–1875.* New York: Scribner's.

———. 1992. *Nations and Nationalism since 1780.* Cambridge, U.K.: Cambridge University Press.

Hodges, Donald C., and Robert Elias Abu Shanab, eds. 1972. *NLF: National Liberation Fronts, 1960/1970.* New York: Morrow.

Hooson, David J. M., ed. 2002. *Geography and National Identity.* Malden, Mass.: Blackwell.

Horowitz, Donald L. 1985. *Ethnic Groups in Conflict.* Berkeley: University of California Press.

Horsman, A., and A. Marshall. 1994. *After the Nation State.* London: HarperCollins.

Hossay, Patrick. 2002. *Contentions of Nationhood: Nationalist Movements, Political Conflict, and Social Changes in Flanders, Scotland, and French Canada.* Lanham, Md.: Lexington.

Hurewitz, J. C. 1968. *The Struggle for Palestine.* New York: Greenwood.

Hussein, Mahmoud. 1973. *Class Conflict in Egypt, 1945–1970.* New York: Monthly Review Press.

Hutchinson, John, and Anthony D. Smith, eds. 1994. *Nationalism.* New York: Oxford University Press.

———, eds. 2002. *Nationalism: Critical Concepts in Political Science.* New York: Routledge.

Ibrahim, Ferhad. 1995. "The Kurdish National Movement and the Struggle for National Autonomy." In *The National Question: Nationalism, Ethnic Conflict, and Self-Determination in the Twentieth Century*, ed. Berch Berberoglu. Philadelphia: Temple University Press.

———, and Gulistan Gurbey, eds. 2001. *The Kurdish Conflict in Turkey.* London: Palgrave Macmillan.

Ignazi, Piero. 2003. *Extreme Right Parties in Western Europe.* Oxford, U.K.: Oxford University Press.

Ismael, Tareq Y. 1976. *The Arab Left.* Syracuse, N.Y.: Syracuse University Press.

Jacquin-Berdal, Dominique. 2003. *Nationalism and Ethnicity in the Horn of Africa: A Critique of the Ethnic Interpretation.* Lewiston, N.Y.: Edwin Mellen.

Jaffrelot, Christophe, ed. 2002. *Pakistan: Nationalism without a Nation?* London: Zed Books.

Jankowski, James P. 2001. *Nasser's Egypt, Arab Nationalism, and the Untied Arab Republic.* Boulder, Colo.: Rienner.

Jayawardena, Kumari. 1986. *Feminism and Nationalism in the Third World.* London: Zed Books.

Jubulis, Mark A. 2001. *Nationalism and Democratic Transition: The Politics of Citizenship and Language in Post-Soviet Latvia.* New York: University Press of America.

Jusdanis, Gregory. 2001 *The Necessary Nation.* Princeton, N.J.: Princeton University Press.

Kang, T. S. 1979. *Nationalism and the Crises of Ethnic Minorities in Asia.* Westport, Conn.: Greenwood.

Kaplan, Jeffrey, and Tore Bjorgo. 1998. *Nation and Race: The Developing Euro-American Racist Subculture.* Boston: Northeastern University Press.

Keating, Michael. 2002. *Nations against the State: The New Politics of Nationalism in Quebec, Catalonia, and Scotland.* London: Macmillan.

———, and John McGarry, eds. 2002. *Minority Nationalism and the Changing International Order.* New York: Oxford University Press.

Kecmanovic, Dusan. 2001. *Ethnic Times: Exploring Ethnonationalism in the Former Yugoslavia.* Westport, Conn.: Praeger.

Keddie, N. 1980. *Iran: Religion, Politics, and Society.* London: Frank Cass.

———. 1981. *Roots of Revolution: An Interpretive History of Modern Iran.* New Haven, Conn.: Yale University Press.

———, and E. Hooglund, eds. 1982. *The Iranian Revolution and the Islamic Republic.* Washington, D.C.: Middle East Institute.

Kedourie, Elie. 1993. *Nationalism.* 4th ed. Malden, Mass.: Blackwell.

Kenane, Derek. 1964. *The Kurds and Kurdistan.* London: Oxford University Press.

Khalidi, Rashid, Lisa Anderson, Muhammad Muslih, and Reeva S. Simon, eds. 1991. *The Origins of Arab Nationalism.* New York: Columbia University Press.

Kidd, Colin. 1999. *British Identities before Nationalism: Ethnicity and Nationhood in the Atlantic World, 1600–1800.* Cambridge, U.K.: Cambridge University Press.

Kimmerling, Baruch, and Joel S. Migdal. 1993. *Palestinians: The Making of a People.* New York: Free Press.

———. 2003. *The Palestinian People: A History.* Cambridge, Mass.: Harvard University Press.

Kirisci, Kemal, and Gareth M. Winrow. 1997. *The Kurdish Question and Turkey: An Example of Trans-State Ethnic Conflict.* London: Frank Cass.

Knapp, Peter, and Alan J. Spector. 1991. *Crisis and Change.* Chicago: Nelson Hall Publishers.

Kohn, Hans. 1944. *The Idea of Nationalism.* New York: Collier Books.

———. 1962. *The Age of Nationalism.* New York: Harper.

———. 1965. *Nationalism: Its Meaning and History.* Princeton, N.J.: Van Nostrand.

Koohi-Kamali, Farideh. 2004. *The Political Development of the Kurds in Iran: Pastoral Nationalism.* London: Palgrave Macmillan.

Krapauskas, Virgil. 2000. *Nationalism and Historiography.* New York: Columbia University Press.

Laughlin, Jim Mac. 2000. *Reimagining the Nation State: The Contested Terrains of Irish Nation Building.* London: Pluto Press.

Laurin-Frenette, N. 1978. *Production de l'Etat et Formes de la Nation.* Montréal: Nouvelle Optique.

Lazarus, Neil. 1999. *Nationalism and Cultural Practice in the Postcolonial World.* Cambridge, U.K.: Cambridge University Press.

Leifer, Michael, ed. 2000. *Asian Nationalism.* New York: Routledge.

Lenin, V. I. 1960. "Imperialism: The Highest Stage of Capitalism." In *Selected Works*, Vol. 1. Moscow: Foreign Languages Publishing House.

——. 1964a. "Critical Remarks on the National Question." In *Collected Works*. Vol. 20. Moscow: Progress Publishers.

——. 1964b. "The Right of Nations to Self-Determination." In *Collected Works*. Vol. 20. Moscow: Progress Publishers.

——. 1964. "The Socialist Revolution and the Right of Nations to Self-Determination: Theses." In *Collected Works*, Vol. 22. Moscow: Progress Publishers.

——. 1966. "Preliminary Draft Theses on the National and the Colonial Questions." In *Collected Works*, Vol. 31. Moscow: Progress Publishers.

——. 1966. "The Question of Nationalities or 'Autonomisation'." In *Collected Works*, Vol. 36. Moscow: Progress Publishers.

——. 1974. "The State." In K. Marx, F. Engels, and V. I. Lenin, *On Historical Materialism*. New York: International Publishers.

Lentin, Alana. 2004. *Racism and Anti-Racism in Europe*. London: Pluto Press.

Leoussi, Athena S., and Anthony D. Smith. 2001. *Encyclopedia of Nationalism*. New Brunswick, N.J.: Transaction.

Levkovsky, A. I. 1966. *Capitalism in India*. Delhi: People's Publishing House.

Lockman, Zachary, and Joel Beinin. 1989. *Intifada: The Palestinian Uprising against Israeli Occupation*. Boston: South End Press.

Longuenesse, Elizabeth. 1979. "The Class Nature of the State in Syria." *MERIP Reports* 9, no. 4 (May).

López, José A. 1977. *Puerto Rican Nationalism: A Reader*. Chicago: Editorial Coqui.

Löwy, Michael. 1976. "Marxism and the National Question." *New Left Review* no. 96.

Luoug, Pauline Jones, ed. 2004. *The Transformation of Central Asia: States and Societies from Soviet Rule to Independence*. Ithaca, N.Y.: Cornell University Press.

Luxemburg, Rosa. 1976. *The National Question: Selected Writings of Rosa Luxemburg*. Edited and with an introduction by Horace B. Davis. New York: Monthly Review Press.

Magee, John. 1974. *Northern Ireland: Crisis and Conflict*. London: Routledge & Kegan Paul.

Maldonado-Denis, Manuel. 1972. *Puerto Rico: A Socio-Historic Interpretation*. Trans. by Elena Vialo. New York: Random House.

——. 1976. "Prospects for Latin American Nationalism: The Case of Puerto Rico." *Latin American Perspectives* 3, no. 3.

Malesevic, Sinisa. 2002. *Ideology, Legitimacy, and the New State: Yugoslavia, Serbia, and Croatia*. London: Frank Cass.

——, and Mark Haugaard, eds. 2002. *Making Sense of Collectivity: Ethnicity, Nationalism and Globalization*. London: Pluto Press.

Malik, Iftikhar Haider. 1999. *Islam, Nationalism and the West: Issues of Identity in Pakistan*. Hampshire, U.K.: Palgrave Macmillan.

Mann, Susan. 2003. *The Dream of Nation*. Toronto: McGill-Queens University Press.

Marger, Martin N. 2000. *Race and Ethnic Relations: American and Global Perspectives*. 5th ed. Belmont, Calif.: Wadsworth.

Marks, Shula, and Stanley Tarpido, eds. 1987. *The Politics of Race, Class, and Nationalism in Twentieth Century South Africa*. London: Longman.

Marvin, Carolyn, and David W. Ingle. 1999. *Blood Sacrifice and the Nation: Totem Rituals and the American Flag*. Cambridge, U.K.: Cambridge University Press.

Marx, Anthony W. 2003a. *Faith in Nation/Bound by Hatred*. London: Oxford University Press.

———. 2003b. *Faith in Nation: Exclusionary Origins of Nationalism*. Oxford, U.K.: Oxford University Press.

Marx, Karl, and Frederick Engels. 1947. *The German Ideology*. New York: International Publishers.

———. 1972a. "Manifesto of the Communist Party." In K. Marx and F. Engels, *Selected Works*. New York: International Publishers.

———. 1972b. *On Colonialism*. New York: International Publishers.

Masalha, Nur. 1992. *Expulsion of the Palestinians*. Washington, D.C.: Institute for Palestine Studies.

Maybury-Lewis, David. 1997. *Indigenous Peoples, Ethnic Groups, and the State*. Boston: Allyn and Bacon.

Mayer, Tamar, ed. 1999. *Gender Ironies of Nationalism: Sexing the Nation*. New York: Routledge.

McDowall, David. 1989. *Palestine and Israel: The Uprising and Beyond*. Berkeley: University of California Press.

———. 1992. *The Kurds: A Nation Denied*. London: Minority Rights Group.

———. 1995. *The Palestinians: The Road to Nationhood*. London: Minority Rights Group.

———. 1996. *A Modern History of the Kurds*. London: I. B. Tauris.

McGarry, John, and Brendan O'Leary, eds. 1990. *The Future of Northern Ireland*. Oxford, U.K.: Clarendon Press.

McPherson, James M. 1999. *Is Blood Thicker Than Water?: Crises of Nationalism in the Modern World*. Vancouver: Vintage.

McRoberts, K., and D. Posgate. 1976. *Quebec: Social Change and Political Crisis*. Toronto: McClelland and Stewart.

McRoberts, Kenneth. 2001. *Catalonia: Nation Building without a State*. London: Oxford University Press.

McVeigh, Brian J. 2004. *Nationalisms of Japan: Managing and Mystifying Identity*. Lanham, Md.: Rowman & Littlefield.

Meyer, Brigit, and Peter Geschiere, eds. 1999. *Globalization and Identity: Dialectics of Flow and Closure*. Malden, Mass.: Blackwell.

Miliband, Ralph, and Leo Panitch, eds. 1994. *Socialist Register 1994: Between Globalism and Nationalism*. London: Merlin.

Miller, David. 1999. *On Nationality*. London: Clarendon Press.

Miller, Norman, and Roderick Aya, eds. 1971. *National Liberation: Revolution in the Third World*. New York: Free Press.

Minogue, Kenneth R. 1967. *Nationalism*. London: Batsford.

Miscevic, Nenad, ed. 2000. *Nationalism and Ethnic Conflict: Philosophical Perspectives*. Chicago: Open Court.

Moaddel, M. 1992. "Ideology as Episodic Discourse: The Case of the Iranian Revolution." *American Sociological Review* 57 (June).

————. 1993. *Class, Politics, and Ideology in the Iranian Revolution*. New York: Columbia University Press.

Moghadam, Valentine M. 1989. "Populist Revolution and the Islamic State in Iran." In *Revolution in the World System*, ed. T. Boswell. Westport, Conn.: Greenwood.

————. 1994a. *Gender and National Identity: Women and Politics in Muslim Societies*. London: Zed Books.

————. 1994b. "Islamic Populism, Class, and Gender in Postrevolutionary Iran." In *A Century of Revolution: Social Movements in Iran*, ed. J. Foran. Minneapolis: University of Minnesota Press

Moore, Margaret. 2002. *The Ethics of Nationalism*. New York: Oxford University Press.

Morison, John, ed. 2000. *Ethnic and National Issues in Russian and East European History*. Hampshire, U.K.: Palgrave Macmillan.

Morris, Benny. 2001. *Righteous Victims: A History of the Zionist–Arab Conflict, 1881–2001*. New York: Knopf.

Motyl, Alexander, ed. 2002. *Encyclopedia of Nationalism*. San Diego: Academic.

Moulder, Frances V. 1977. *Japan, China and the Modern World Economy*. Cambridge, U.K.: Cambridge University Press.

Müge Göcek, Fatma. 2002. *Social Constructions of Nationalism in the Middle East*. Albany: State University of New York Press.

Mukherjee, Aditya. 2002. *Imperialism, Nationalism and the Making of the Indian Capitalist Class, 1920–1947*. Thousand Oaks, Calif.: Sage.

Musgrave, Thomas D. 2000. *Self-Determination and National Minorities*. New York: Oxford University Press.

Nairn, Tom. 1981. *The Break-Up of Britain*. 2nd ed. London: Verso.

Nandy, Ashis. 1994. *The Illegitimacy of Nationalism*. Delhi: Oxford University Press.

Nayar, Baldev Raj. 2001. *Globalization and Nationalism: The Changing Balance in India's Economic Policy, 1950–2000*. Thousand Oaks, Calif.: Sage.

Neumann, Franz L. 1944. *Behemoth: The Structure and Practice of National Socialism, 1933–1944*. New York: Harper & Row.

Nicholson, Philip Yale. 2001. *Who Do We Think We Are?: Race and Nation in the Modern World*. Armonk, N.Y.: Sharpe.

Nimni, Ephraim. 1991. *Marxism and Nationalism: Theoretical Origins of a Political Crisis*. London: Pluto Press.

Nkrumah, Kwame. 1965. *Neo-Colonialism: The Last Stage of Imperialism*. New York: International Publishers.

————. 1969. *Handbook of Revolutionary Warfare*. New York: International Publishers.

Olson, Robert. 1989. *The Emergence of Kurdish Nationalism and the Sheikh Said Rebellion, 1880–1925*. Austin: University of Texas Press.

————, ed. 1996. *The Kurdish Nationalist Movement in the 1990s*. Lexington: The University Press of Kentucky.

Omvedt, Gail. 1975. "Caste, Class and Women's Liberation in India." *Bulletin of Concerned Asian Scholars* 7, no. 1.

Oommen, T. K., ed. 1997. *Citizenship and National Identity*. New Delhi: Sage.

Ortakovski, Vladimir. 2000. *Minorities in the Balkans*. Ardsley, N.Y.: Transnational.

O'Sullivan See, Katherine. 1986. *First World Nationalisms: Class and Ethnic Politics in Northern Ireland and Quebec*. Chicago: University of Chicago Press.

Özkirimli, Umut. 2000. *Theories of Nationalism: A Critical Introduction*. New York: St. Martin's.

Özoglu, Hakan. 2004. *Kurdish Notables and the Ottoman State: Evolving Identities, Competing Loyalties, and Shifting Boundaries*. Albany: State University of New York Press.

Panitch, Leo. 1977. *The Canadian State*. Toronto: University of Toronto Press.

Pappe, Ilan. 2004. *A History of Modern Palestine: One Land, Two Peoples*. Cambridge, U.K.: Cambridge University Press.

Parsa, M. 1989. *The Social Origins of the Iranian Revolution*. New Brunswick, N.J.: Rutgers University Press.

Patterson, Henry. 1989. "Ireland: A New Phase in the Conflict Between Nationalism and Unionism." *Science & Society* 53, no. 2 (Summer).

Paul, T. V., G. John Ikenberry, and John A. Hall, eds. 2003. *The Nation-State in Question*. Princeton, N.J.: Princeton University Press.

Pavkovic, Aleksandar. 2000a. *The Fragmentation of Yugoslavia: Nationalism and War in the Balkans*. Hampshire, U.K.: Palgrave Macmillan.

———. 2000b. *The Fragmentation of Yugoslavia: Nationalism and War in the Balkans*. New York: St. Martin's.

Pearlman, Wendy. 2003. *Occupied Voices: Stories of Everyday Life from the Second Intifada*. New York: Thunder's Mouth Press/Nation Books.

Perica, Vjekoslav. 2002. *Balkan Idols: Religion and Nationalism in Yugoslav States*. New York: Oxford University Press.

Pesaran, M. H. 1982. "The System of Dependent Capitalism in Pre- and Post-Revolutionary Iran." *International Journal of Middle East Studies* 14.

Peteet, Julie. 1989. "Women and National Politics in the Middle East." In *Power and Stability in the Middle East*, ed. Berch Berberoglu. London: Zed Books.

Phadnis, Urmila, and Rajat Ganguly. 2002. *Ethnicity and Nation-Building in South Asia*. Thousand Oaks, Calif.: Sage.

Philipp, Thomas. 1980. "Feminism and Nationalism in Egypt." In *Women in the Muslim World*, ed. Lois Beck and Nikki Keddie. Cambridge, Mass.: Harvard University Press.

Pinard, M., and R. Hamilton. 1984. "The Class Bases of the Quebec Independence Movement." *Ethnic and Racial Studies* 7, no. 1 (January).

Pool, James, and Suzanne Pool. 1978. *Who Financed Hitler: The Secret Funding of Hitler's Rise to Power, 1919–1933*. New York: Dial Press.

Poole, Ross. 1999. *Nation and Identity*. New York: Routledge.

Poulantzas, Nicos. 1974. *Political Power and Social Classes*. London: New Left Books.

Pratt, Jeff. 2003. *Class, Nation, and Identity*. London: Pluto Press.

Pratt, Jeff C. 2003. *Class and Nationalist Movements in Europe*. London: Pluto Press.

Probert, Belinda. 1978. *Beyond Orange and Green: The Political Economy of the Northern Ireland Crisis*. London: Zed Books.

Quintero-Rivera, Angel. 1979. "Imperialism and Class Struggle in Puerto Rico." *Two Thirds* 2, no. 1.

———. 1980. "Notes on Puerto Rican National Development: Class and Nation in a Colonial Context." *Marxist Perspectives* 3, no. 1.

Rajagopalan, Swarna. 2001. *State and Nation in South Asia*. Boulder, Colo.: Rienner.

Ranchod-Nilsson, Sita, and Mary Ann Tetreault, eds. 2000. *Women, States and Nationalism: At Home in the Nation?* New York: Routledge.

Reich, Wilhelm. 1970. *The Mass Psychology of Fascism*. New York: Noonday Press.

Reicher, Stephen, and Nick Hopkins. 2001. *Self and Nation: Categorization, Contestation and Mobilization*. Thousand Oaks, Calif.: Sage.

Reilly, James. 1982. "Israel in Lebanon, 1975–82." *MERIP Reports* 12, nos. 6–7 (September–October).

Renan, Ernest. 1994 [1882]. "Qu'est-ce qu'une nation?" Excerpted in *Nationalism*, ed. John Hutchinson and Anthony D. Smith. New York: Oxford University Press.

Rigby, Andrew. 1991. *Living the Intifada*. London: Zed Books.

Rodney, Walter. 1972. *How Europe Underdeveloped Africa*. London and Dar es Salaam: Tanzania Publishing House and Bogle L'Ouverture Publications.

Roshwald, Aviel. 2001. *Ethnic Nationalism and the Fall of Empires: Central Europe, Russia and the Middle East, 1914–1923*. New York: Routledge.

Roudometof, Victor. 2002. *Collective Memory, National Identity, and Ethnic Conflict: Greece, Bulgaria, and the Macedonian Question*. Westport, Conn.: Praeger.

Rudolph, Joseph, Jr., ed. 2003. *Encyclopedia of Modern Ethnic Conflicts*. Westport, Conn.: Greenwood.

Said, Edward W. 1994. *The Politics of Dispossession: The Struggle for Palestinian Self-Determination, 1969–1994*. New York: Pantheon.

Sayigh, Rosemary. 1979. *Palestinians: From Peasants to Revolutionaries*. London: Zed Books.

———. 1994. *Too Many Enemies: The Palestinian Experience in Lebanon*. London: Zed Books.

Schulze, Hagen. 1996. *States, Nations and Nationalism*. Malden, Mass.: Blackwell.

Schweitzer, Arthur. 1964. *Big Business and the Third Reich*. Bloomington: Indiana University Press.

Searle-White, Joshua. 2001. *The Psychology of Nationalism*. Hampshire, U.K.: Palgrave Macmillan.

Seth, Sanjay. 1995. *Marxist Theory and Nationalist Politics*. New Delhi: Sage.

Sethi, Rumina. 1999. *Myths of the Nation: National Identity and Literary Representation*. Gloucestershire, U.K.: Claredon.

Seton-Watson, H. 1977. *Nations and States*. London: Methuen.

Sfikas, Thanasis D., and Christopher Williams, eds. 1999. *Ethnicity and Nationalism in East Central Europe and the Balkans*. Sudbury, Mass.: Dartmouth.

Sharabi, Hisham B., ed. 1966. *Nationalism and Revolution in the Arab World*. Princeton, N.J.: Van Nostrand.

Sheth, D. L. 1989. "State, Nations and Ethnicity: Experiences of Third World Countries." *Economic and Political Weekly* 24.

Smith, Anthony, Obi Igwara, Athena Leoussi, and Terry Mulhall, eds., 1995. "Editorial." *Nations and Nationalism* 1, no. 1.

Smith, Anthony D. 1981. *The Ethnic Revival*. New York: Cambridge University Press.

——. 1983. *Theories of Nationalism*. 2nd ed. New York: Holmes and Meier.

——. 1986. *The Ethnic Origins of Nations*. Oxford, U.K.: Blackwell.

——. 1991. *National Identity*. London: Penguin.

——. 1999. *Myths and Memories of the Nation*. New York: Oxford University Press.

——. 2000. *The Nation in History: Historiographical Debates about Ethnicity and Nationalism*. Hanover, N.H.: University Press of New England.

——. 2001. *Nationalism: Theory, Ideology, History*. Cambridge, U.K.: Polity Press.

Smith, Jeremy. 1999. *The Bolsheviks and the National Question, 1917–23*. Hampshire, U.K.: Palgrave Macmillan.

Smith, Pamela Ann. 1989. "Palestine and the Palestinians." In *Power and Stability in the Middle East*, ed. Berch Berberoglu. London: Zed Books.

Snyder, Louis L. 1954. *The Meaning of Nationalism*. New Brunswick, N.J.: Rutgers University Press.

——. 1990. *Encyclopedia of Nationalism*. New York: Paragon House.

——, ed. 1964. *The Dynamics of Nationalism*. Princeton, N.J.: Van Nostrand.

Stalin, Joseph. 1934. *Marxism and the National Question*. New York: International Publishers.

Starrs, Roy, ed. 2002. *Nations under Siege: Globalization and Nationalism in Asia*. New York: St. Martin's.

Stork, Joe. 1989. "Class, State, and Politics in Iraq." In *Power and Stability in the Middle East*, ed. Berch Berberoglu. London: Zed Books.

Stein, Stanley J., and Barbara H. Stein. 1970. *The Colonial Heritage of Latin America*. New York: Oxford University Press.

Sugar, Peter F. 1999. *East European Nationalism, Politics and Religion*. Burlington, Vt.: Ashgate.

——, ed. 1995. *East European Nationalism in the Twentieth Century*. New York: University Press of America.

Suny, Ronald. 1990. "The Revenge of the Past: Socialism and Ethnic Conflict in Transcaucasia." *New Left Review* 184 (October–November).

——. 1991. "Incomplete Revolution: National Movements and the Collapse of the Soviet Empire." *New Left Review* 189 (September–October).

Suny, Ronald Grigor, and Terry Martin, eds. *A State of Nations: Empire and Nation Making in the Age of Lenin and Stalin*. New York: Oxford University Press.

Suny, Ronald Grigor, and Michael D. Kennedy, eds. 2001. *Intellectuals and the Articulation of the Nation*. Ann Arbor: University of Michigan Press.

Suter, Keith. 2003. *Global Order and Global Disorder: Globalization and the Nation-State*. Westport, Conn.: Praeger.

Suzman, Mark. 1999. *Ethnic Nationalism and State Power: The Rise of Irish Nationalism, Afrikaner Nationalism and Zionism*. Hampshire, U.K.: Palgrave Macmillan.

Szymanski, Albert. 1978. *The Capitalist State and the Politics of Class*. Cambridge, Mass.: Winthrop Publishers.

——. 1981. *The Logic of Imperialism*. New York: Praeger.

——. 1983. *Class Structure: A Critical Perspective*. New York: Praeger.

Tamari, Salim, ed. 1982. "Factionalism and Class Formation in Recent Palestinian History." In *Studies in the Economic and Social History of Palestine in the Nineteenth and Twentieth Centuries*, ed. Roger Owen. London: Macmillan.

Taras, Ray, and Rajat Ganguly. 2001. *Understanding Ethnic Conflict: The International Dimension*. 2nd ed. London: Longman.

Tasca, Angelo. 1966. *The Rise of Italian Fascism 1918–1922*. New York: Fertig.

Teichova, Alice, and Herbert Matis, eds. 2003. *Nation, State, and the Economy in History*. Cambridge, U.K.: Cambridge University Press.

——, and Jaroslav Patek, eds. 2001. *Economic Change and the National Question in Twentieth-Century Europe*. Cambridge, U.K.: Cambridge University Press.

Therborn, Goran. 1976. *Science, Class and Society*. London: New Left Books.

——. 1978. *What Does the Ruling Class Do When It Rules?* London: New Left Books.

Thom, Martin. 1995. *Republics, Nations and Tribes*. London: Verso.

Thomas, Raju G. C., ed. 2003. *Yugoslavia Unraveled: Sovereignty, Self-Determination, Intervention*. Lanham, Md.: Lexington.

Tilly, Charles, ed. 1975. *The Formation of National States in Western Europe*. Princeton, N.J.: Princeton University Press.

——. 1995. *Citizenship, Identity, and Social History*. Cambridge, U.K.: Cambridge University Press.

——. 2003. *The Politics of Collective Violence*. Cambridge, U.K.: Cambridge University Press.

Toft, Monica Duffy, 1965. 2003. *The Geography of Ethnic Violence: Identity, Interests, and the Indivisibility of Territory*. Princeton, N.J.: Princeton University Press.

Triandafyllidou, Anna. 2002. *Negotiating Nationhood in a Changing Europe: Views from the Press*. Lewiston, N.Y.: Mellen.

Tsokhas, Kosmas. 2002. *Making a Nation State: Cultural Identity, Economic Nationalism and Sexuality in Australian History*. Melbourne, Australia: Melbourne University Press.

Tuminez, Astrid S. 2000. *Russian Nationalism since 1856*. Lanham, Md.: Rowman & Littlefield.

Turok, Ben. 1980. *Revolutionary Thought in the Twentieth Century*. London: Zed Books.

Udovicki, Jasminka. 1995. "Nationalism, Ethnic Conflict, and Self-Determination in the Former Yugoslavia." In *The National Question: Nationalism, Ethnic Conflict, and Self-Determination in the Twentieth Century*, ed. Berch Berberoglu. Philadelphia: Temple University Press.

Van Diepen, Maria, ed. 1988. *The National Question in South Africa*. London: Zed Books.

Van Horne, Winston A., ed. 1999. *Global Convulsions: Race, Ethnicity, and Nationalism at the End of the Twentieth Century*. Albany: State University of New York Press.

Vanley, Ismet Sheriff. 1971. *Survey of the National Question of Turkish Kurdistan with Historical Background*. Zurich: Hevra.

Van Schendel, Willem, and Erik J. Zurcher, eds. 2001. *Identity Politics in Central Asia and the Muslim World: Nationalism, Ethnicity and Labour in the Twentieth Century*. New York: I. B. Tauris.

Vilar, Pierre. 1979. "On Nations and Nationalism." *Marxist Perspectives* 2, no. 1.

Vincent, Andrew. 2002. *Nationalism and Particularity*. Cambridge, U.K.: Cambridge University Press.

Walshe, Peter. 1970. *The Rise of African Nationalism in South Africa: The African National Congress, 1912–1952*. Berkeley: University of California Press.

Weber, Max. 1946. *From Max Weber: Essays in Sociology*. Edited by H. H. Gerth and C. Wright Mills. New York: Oxford University Press.

Wei, C. X. George, and Xiaoyuan Liu, eds. 2001. *Chinese Nationalism in Perspective: Historical and Recent Cases*. Westport, Conn.: Greenwood.

Welty, Gordon. 1987. "Progressive Versus Reactive Nationalism." In *Arab Nationalism and the Future of the Arab World*, ed. Hani Faris. Belmont, Mass.: Association of Arab-American University Graduates.

———. 1995. "Palestinian Nationalism and the Struggle for National Self-Determination." In *The National Question: Nationalism, Ethnic Conflict and Self-Determination in the Twentieth Century*, ed. Berch Berberoglu. Philadelphia: Temple University Press.

Westwood, Sallie, and Annie Phizacklea. 2001. *Trans-Nationalism and the Politics of Belonging*. New York: Routledge.

White, George W. 2000. *Nationalism and Territory*. Boulder, Colo.: Rowman & Littlefield.

Williams, Christopher, and Thanassis D. Sfikas, eds. 1999. *Ethnicity and Nationalism in Russia, the CIS and the Baltic States*. Burlington, Vt.: Ashgate.

Williams, Eric. 1966. *Capitalism and Slavery*. Reprint. New York: Capricorn.

Wilson, Sandra, ed. 2002. *Nation and Nationalism in Japan*. New York: Routledge.

Wilson, Thomas M., and Hastings Donnan. 1998. *Border Identities: Nation and State at International Frontiers*. Cambridge, U.K.: Cambridge University Press.

Wimmer, Andreas. 2002. *Nationalist Exclusion and Ethnic Conflict: Shadows of Modernity*. Cambridge, U.K.: Cambridge University Press.

Yermakova, Antonina, and Valentin Ratnikov. 1986. *What Are Classes and the Class Struggle?* Moscow: Progress Publishers.

Yeros, Paris, ed. 1999. *Ethnicity and Nationalism in Africa: Constructivist Reflections and Contemporary Politics*. Hampshire, U.K.: Palgrave Macmillan.

Yohannes, Okbazghi. 2001. *Political Economy of an Authoritarian Modern State and Religious Nationalism in Egypt*. Lewiston, N.Y.: Edwin Mellen.

Yoshino, Kosaku, ed. 2000. *Consuming Ethnicity and Nationalism: Asian Experiences*. Honolulu: University of Hawaii Press.

Young, Gay, and Bette J. Dickerson. 1994. *Color, Class, and Country*. London: Zed Books.

Younis, Mona, N. 2000. *Liberation and Democratization: The South African and Palestinian National Movements*. Minneapolis: University of Minnesota Press.

Zagladin, V., ed. 1975. *The Revolutionary Movement of Our Time and Nationalism*. Moscow: Progress Publishers.

Zavareei, M. 1982. "Dependent Capitalist Development in Iran and the Mass Uprising of 1979." *Research in Political Economy* 5.

Zolner, Mette. 2000. *Re-Imagining the Nation: Debates on Immigrants, Identities and Memories*. New York: Peter Lang.

Index

About the Author

Berch Berberoglu is Foundation Professor and Director of Graduate Studies in the Department of Sociology at the University of Nevada, Reno, where he has been teaching and conducting research for the past twenty-six years.

Dr. Berberoglu has authored and edited twenty-one books and many articles in numerous scholarly journals. His recent books include *Class Structure and Social Transformation* (Praeger), *The National Question: Nationalism, Ethnic Conflict, and Self-Determination in the Twentieth Century* (Temple University Press), *Turmoil in the Middle East: Imperialism, War and Political Instability* (State University of New York Press), *Labor and Capital in the Age of Globalization* (Rowman & Littlefield), and *The Globalization of Capital and the Nation-State* (Rowman & Littlefield). He is currently doing research and writing for his next book, *The State and Revolution in the Twentieth Century*.

Dr. Berberoglu received his Ph.D. from the University of Oregon in 1977 and his B.S. and M.A. from Central Michigan University in 1972 and 1974.